Historical Wig Styling:
Ancient Egypt to the 1830s

THE FOCAL PRESS COSTUME TOPICS SERIES

Costumes are one of the most important aspects of any production. They are essential tools that create a new reality for both the actor and audience member, which is why you want them to look flawless! Luckily, we're here to help with The Focal Press Costume Topics Series; offering books that explain how to design, construct, and accessorize costumes from a variety of genres and time periods. Step-by-step projects ensure you never get lost or lose inspiration for your design. Let us lend you a hand (or a needle or a comb) with your next costume endeavor!

Titles in The Focal Press Costume Topics Series:

The Focal Press Costume Topics Series
HISTORICAL WIG STYLING
{ Ancient Egypt to the 1830s }
Allison Lowery

The Focal Press Costume Topics Series
HISTORICAL WIG STYLING
{ Victorian to the Present }
Allison Lowery

The Focal Press Costume Topics Series
DRAPING PERIOD COSTUMES
{ Classical Greek to Victorian }
Sharon Sobel

Historical Wig Styling:
Ancient Egypt to the 1830s

Allison Lowery

Focal Press
Taylor & Francis Group

NEW YORK AND LONDON

First published 2013
by Focal Press
70 Blanchard Rd Suite 402
Burlington, MA 01803

Simultaneously published in the UK
by Focal Press
2 Park Square, Milton Park, Abingdon, Oxon OX14 4RN

Focal Press is an imprint of the Taylor & Francis Group, an Informa business

Notices
Knowledge and best practice in this field are constantly changing. As new research
and experience broaden our understanding, changes in research methods, professional
practices, or medical treatment may become necessary.

Practitioners and researchers must always rely on their own experience and knowledge
in evaluating and using any information, methods, compounds, or experiments
described herein. In using such information or methods they should be mindful of
their own safety and the safety of others, including parties for whom they have a
professional responsibility.

Product or corporate names may be trademarks or registered trademarks, and are used
only for identification and explanation without intent to infringe.

Library of Congress Cataloging in Publication Data
Lowery, Allison.
Historical wig styling. Ancient Egypt to the 1830s / Allison Lowery.
pages cm
Includes bibliographical references.
1. Wigs--Design and construction. 2. Hairdressing. 3. Hairstyles--History.
4. Theatrical wigs. I. Title.
TT975.L83 2013
792.02'7--dc23
2012034032

ISBN: 978-0-240-82123-8 (pbk)
ISBN: 978-0-240-82140-5 (ebk)

Typeset in Adobe Garamond
By TNQ Books and Journals, Chennai, India

Printed by 1010 PrintingInternational Limited

{ *contents* }

{ *Acknowledgments* }

So many people have helped to make this book possible. Many heartfelt thanks go out to the amazing Stacey Walker, Emma Elder and the staff at Focal Press/Taylor and Francis; Kristina Tollefson, technical editor/reader of the highest quality; Texas Performing Arts and the Texas Performing Arts Costume Shop, especially Kathy Panoff and Patricia Risser; the University of Texas Department of Theatre and Dance; Wendy Zieger and the Bridgeman Art Library; Wikipedia Commons; Everything Vintage; my teachers and mentors, Martha Ruskai and Patricia Wesp; the insanely amazing Tim Babiak for the most rocking amazing photography and collaboration anyone could ask for; the models—Emma Dirks, Anna Fugate, Leslie Hethcox, Ariel Livingston, Sabrina Lotfi, Marsherrie Madkins, Josephine McAdam, and Ivy Negron—for being incredible style chameleons; my students—Tara Cooper, Emma Dirks, Anna Fugate, Thumper Gosney, Beauty Kampf-Thibodeau, Josephine McAdam, Kara Meche, Lexi O'Reilly, Bethany Renfro, Maur Sela, Sarah Shade, and Elisa Solomon, for being a constant source of inspiration; Stephanie Williams Caillabet; Amanda French; Darren Jinks; Rick Jarvic; Susan Branch Towne; Dennis and Jeffrey at Elsen Associates; the Friday Night Gamers—Terry, Sheena, Jeff, Sam, Charles, Brad, Chris, and Irving; the TXRD Lonestar Rollergirls (Cherry Bombs destroy!); the TXRD BWs, especially Pinto, Sheryl, Chicago Jimmy, Sword, Amy, and Mama Peno; Jim's Restaurant; Dave and Patti; *Cher* Uncle, Arthur Hall Smith, for helping to give me my love of art; my brother, Scott; my grandparents, Jack and Elizabeth Karnes (Grandma, you will always be my favorite 1940s redhead–RIP); Mom (thank you for the never ending love and encouragement) and Dad (how I wish you could have seen this finished); and especially to Terry, without whose love and support this book would not have been finished.

—Allison Lowery

one

INTRODUCTION TO WIG STYLING TECHNIQUES

Figure 1.1   Wig styling student Maur Sela works on styling a lace front wig.

Welcome to the wonderful and sometime mysterious world of wig styling! Wigs can be a great asset to any theatrical costume or historical costume recreation. Learning the techniques of wig styling can help everyone achieve the completely authentic look they are striving for. Wigs give you the ability to create many looks that would take a long time to create with someone's real hair—wigs have the advantage of being able to be prepped ahead of time so that they are ready to put on at a moment's notice, which saves valuable time with your performer! This is especially helpful if you are working on a theatrical production and you only have an hour and a half to get a cast of twenty people ready in historical looks. The techniques presented in this book will help you create a wide number of different hairstyles from different eras of history. Many of these techniques can also be adapted for use on someone's real hair if a wig or hairpiece is not an option. I hope this book will be used by theatre technicians, film technicians, historical re-enactors, fashion professionals, hairstylists, cosplayers, and anyone else looking to create unique and elaborate hairstyles.

Tools, Supplies, and Hair Products

There are a number of tools and products you need to assemble before you begin your journey into wig styling. For suggestions about where to find these items, please refer to Appendix 3 at the back of the book. Here is a list of things you will need:

1. Wigs! All kinds! I most often use lace front wigs that have had their front hairline knotted by hand onto fine lace. While I prefer lace front wigs (their realistic look creates the most authentic looking hairstyles), hard front wigs (wigs that are the easiest to find commercially) can be used to great effect as well. I use equal numbers of human hair wigs and synthetic wigs. I prefer human hair wigs for men's wigs, long loose-hanging wigs (human hair has weight that allows it to hang more naturally than synthetic hair), and for situations where there may only be one or two wigs in a production. Synthetic fiber holds its curl better, which makes it ideal for long running shows, outdoor theatre, or shows where there is vigorous physical activity such as dancing or fighting. Human hair wigs are styled by a combination of wetness, heat, and styling products; synthetic wigs are set using steam.

2. A wig block (also sometimes called the head block). A wig block is a canvas head that is made for styling and making wigs. It is made of canvas and filled with sawdust so that the block is sturdy and easy to pin into. Wig blocks are available in a range of head

sizes. It is important to note that Styrofoam heads are not the same as a wig block. Styrofoam heads are best used for storing a wig that has already been styled. Styrofoam shrinks (sometimes extremely) when heat is applied to it. Therefore, attempting to style a wig with heat (either with steam or by putting the head in a warm wig dryer) can cause the Styrofoam head to distort, making it very difficult to continue styling the wig.

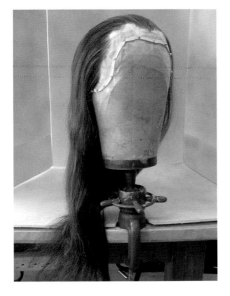

Figure 1.2 A lace front wig on a canvas wig block that is being held onto the table by a wig clamp.

3. A wig clamp. This is a clamp that attaches to the edge of a table so that you may work on your wig without worrying about it falling off of the table. Wig clamps come in both metal and plastic—both work well.

4. Blocking tape. These are pieces of fabric or ribbon that hold the edge of a lace front wig flat while you are working. I prefer to use bias tape or twill tape. Ribbons or shoelaces will also work as blocking tape.

These tapes are also sometimes used to hold a style in place as you work to create waves. Blocking tape can be used over and over again.

5. Pins. You will need two kinds of pins. Blocking pins are the pins you will use to secure the wig to the head block. I prefer to use quilter's pins with round heads, but corsage pins can also be used. These are easy to remove from the block when needed, and their round heads do not snag in the hair when you are styling the wig. You will also need t-pins. These are t-shaped pins that are used to secure rollers to the head. For both blocking pins and t-pins, the longest length you can find is ideal.

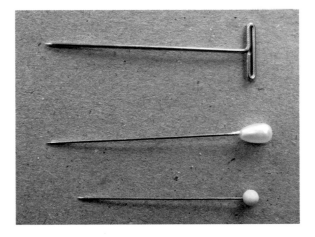

Figure 1.3 From top: a t-pin, a corsage pin, and a round head pin.

6. Rollers. You will need a variety of sizes of rollers. The largest size I use is 1¾ inch diameter rollers. All sizes smaller than that are the most useful. The three sizes I use most often are nickel-sized (7/8 inch diameter), dime-sized (5/8 inch diameter), and pencil-sized (3/8 inch diameter). I use both wire rollers (sometimes called spring wire rollers) and plastic rollers. Wire rollers are easier to pin into when you

are working; otherwise, I have not noticed much difference between them. Note that wire rollers usually come with a bristle brush inside them. I always remove this little brush before using the rollers. I also like to use perm rods for tiny curls.

Figure 1.4   This is a good sample assortment of roller types and sizes.

7. End wraps, also known as end papers. These are used to smooth the ends of the hair so they wrap neatly around the end of the roller. End papers are sold by the box. One box should last you through at least 15 hairstyles.

8. A spray bottle. You will fill the spray bottle with water so that you can wet the wig as you work. Large or small size spray bottles are fine—I prefer large so that I do not have to refill it as often. Other people are more comfortable using a smaller bottle.

9. Combs and brushes. You will also need a variety of combs and brushes to set and style the wig. I consider the following brushes essential:

   • A wide toothed comb. This is used for detangling wet wigs and for combing through hair when a brush would disturb the curl too much.

   • A rat tail comb. These are used for sectioning the hair, making clean parts, and for removing all tangles from the hair.

   • A teasing/smoothing brush. This brush is absolutely essential. It is used for teasing or back-combing the hair, smoothing curls around your finger, controlling flyaway messy hairs, and many other things.

   • A teasing/lifting comb. This comb is not only used to tease hair, but also to lift or "pick out" a voluminous hairstyle so that it is even larger.

   • A large wire brush, often called a cushion brush. This brush is used for brushing through the entire wig once you have removed the rollers. I often use dog brushes for this. I also prefer brushes that do not have tipped bristles. I have found that the tips eventually come off and I end up spending time picking the tips out of the wig.

Figure 1.5   From left to right: a wide-toothed comb, a rat tail comb, a teasing/smoothing brush, a teasing/lifting comb, and a large wire brush.

10. Styling clips. You will need an assortment of small, pronged curl clips (available in both single and double pronged style); long clips that are called either duckbill clips or alligator clips; and butterfly clips. The clips are used to hold sections of hair in place and for pin curl setting.

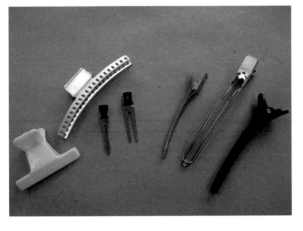

Figure 1.6 From left: butterfly clips, a single-prong curl clip, a double-prong curl clip, and a variety of duckbill/alligator clips.

11. Hair styling pins. You will need a variety of pins once you get to the point of combing out and styling your wig. Black and brown bobby pins, black and bronze hairpins, and three inch hairpins (often referred to as "wig pins") are all necessary. Silver pins can also be useful when you are working with white or grey wigs. It is a good idea to match the color of the pin to the color of the wig you are styling.

12. A wig dryer. Once the wig has been set, it will need to be dried in a wig dryer. There are commercially available wig dryers available for purchase (Figure 1.8).

You can also make your own (Figure 1.9) by putting a hair dryer in a hole cut into a large box (either cardboard or wooden—wood is preferred). An important note: if you do make your own wig dryer, you must keep an eye on it while the hair dryer is on! You do not want the hair dryer to overheat and start a fire. It is also important to make sure that the hair dryer is far enough away from the wig so that the heat from the dryer does not scorch or melt the hair. Angle the hair dryer so that it is not blowing directly on the wig.

13. A small hand steamer. When you are setting a synthetic wig, the curl must be set with steam. A small hand steamer makes it easy to control the direction of the steam and to ensure that every roller is attended to. There are also commercial wig steamers available on the market, but I prefer the smaller hand steamers because they afford more control. Full size steamers and hat steamers also work in a pinch.

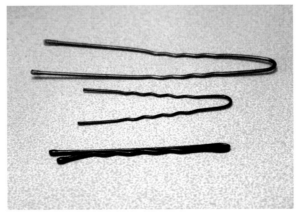

Figure 1.7 From the top: a three-inch wig pin, a hair pin, and a bobby pin.

Figure 1.8   A commercial wig dryer.

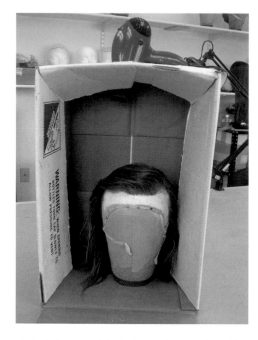

Figure 1.9   A "homemade" wig dryer, using a cardboard box and a commercial hair dryer. The box flaps have been folded in so that the placement of the dryer and the placement of the head block are visible. When you are drying a wig, these flaps should be folded so that the box is closed.

Figuer 1.10   A small hand-held steamer being used to steam a synthetic wig.

14. Hairnets, rubber bands/hair elastics, and rats. Hairnets in a variety of colors will enable you to create long-lasting, neat-looking hairstyles. Rubber bands and/or hair elastics allow you to secure sections of hair and make ponytails and braids. Rats (hair pads) allow you to add fullness to a wig or hairstyle without having to rely on teasing. Rats can be purchased ready made, or can be created by adding loose hair inside a hairnet and rolling it up into the desired size and shape.

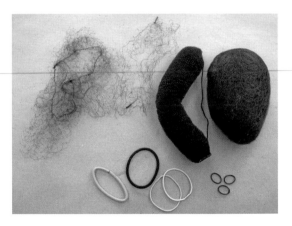

Figure 1.11 An assortment of hairnets, wig rats/pads, and hair elastics.

15. Styling products. I use three different kinds of hair styling products.

    • Hairspray. I prefer aerosol hairspray (as opposed to pump). Whatever brand you prefer is fine.

    • Setting lotion. This lotion is available at beauty supply stores and is used to hold curl and add volume when it is applied to hair as it is being set.

    • Gel. I use the cheapest readily available brand. Gel can also be used as a setting lotion in a pinch. It is also used for slicking down part of a hairstyle.

In general, I avoid styling products that are waxes or pomades. These tend to weight wigs down and make them look clumpy. This can be helpful when you are creating a wig for an unsavory character, but it is more often a hindrance.

16. Hair accessories. Any number of decorative combs, bows, jewelry, flowers, feathers, and other craft supplies can be used to make hair ornaments.

Figure 1.12 An assortment of hair accessories.

17. An apron for covering your clothes. I always wear an apron to help keep hair, water, and styling products off of my clothes.

18. A selection of hairpieces. Hairpieces can be added into wigs that do not have enough hair to create a given style. A variety of colors and sizes of hairpieces is best—wiglets (small, rounded hairpieces), switches (ponytails of hair), and falls (large hairpieces that cover three-quarters of the head) are especially useful.

Figure 1.13   Useful hairpieces, from left: a fall, a switch, and a wiglet.

19. Wefting. Wefting is woven strips of hair used to make wigs, hairpieces, and extensions. Weft can be sewn into wigs to add length or fullness in specific areas.

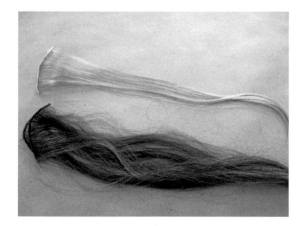

Figure 1.14   Samples of wefting.

20. A selection of wooden or plastic dowel rods, in similar diameter to the rollers you assembled. Dowel rods can be used for pin curl setting, or for helping to shape finished ringlets and curls.

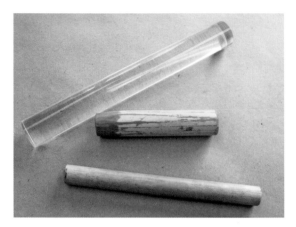

Figure 1.15   A selection of plastic and wooden dowel rods. The yellow rod is a piece of cut-off broom handle—the tapered end helps it to work especially well.

21. A space to work in. Ideally this space will be well ventilated, well lit, and have a good-sized table for your supplies. You can organize your supplies as best suits you. Some people like shelves, some like cabinets, some like rolling carts.

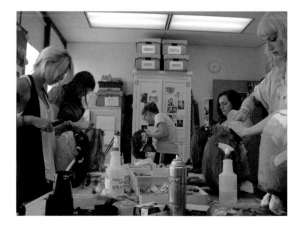

Figure 1.16   University of Texas students Emma Dirks, Bethany Renfro, Lexi O'Reilly, Sarah Thornell, and Lola Hylton at work in the wig room.

Handling Wigs

Once you have assembled all of your supplies and have done your research so that you know all about the style you want to create, you will be ready to begin styling. But where do you start? First, you must learn some basic points about handling wigs.

Human Hair vs Synthetic Hair

The two main materials that the wigs you will be using are made of are human hair and synthetic hair. (Yak wigs are also sometimes used; follow the same rules for handling them as you would for human hair wigs.)

Human hair wigs are made of the hair from, yes, humans. Human hair wigs are set by getting them very wet and then drying them with heat. Hot tools, such as curling irons, flat irons, and crimping irons may be used on human hair wigs. Human hair wigs move more like a real head of hair. Their sheen is more like that of a real head of hair. They are, however, susceptible to bad hair days just like a real person. Human hair wigs are good choices for short men's wigs, long women's wigs that need to look very natural, and wigs that need to last for a long time.

Synthetic wigs are made of plastic hair that is extruded through a machine. Because of this, synthetic hair can be made in any number of lengths and colors. *Synthetic wigs must always be styled with steam!* This includes any kind of curling, waving, or straightening. *No hot tools must ever touch synthetic wigs!* Flat irons, curling irons, and other hot tools will cause the plastic hair of the wig to melt, which will make it useless. Once the hair has been fried, there is nothing you can do to bring it back. All you can do is cut the fried hair out of the wig and replace it with new hair. There are new types of synthetic hair being developed that can withstand styling with hot tools, but unless the wig instructions explicitly say that it can be styled with

heat, you should assume that you cannot do this. Better safe than sorry! Synthetic wigs are a good choice for when you need unusual colors or excessive length. They are also good for a hairstyle that needs to last—this makes them an excellent choice for vigorous musicals or outdoor theatre. Synthetic wigs hold their style very well. They are also significantly cheaper than human hair wigs.

Hard Front Wigs vs Lace Front Wigs

Both synthetic and human hair wigs will come with one of two kinds of front: a hard front or a lace front. A hard front wig is the most common front for the wig to have. This wig has a bound-off fabric edge that finishes off the entire front part of the wig. This often looks artificial and hard, which is why it is called a hard front. If you are using a hard front wig, you will need to do some tricks to soften the hairstyle around the face so that it looks more natural on the performer. Lace front wigs are wigs that have had the hard front of the wig cut off. The front edge of the wig then has a piece of almost invisible fine lace, known as wig lace, sewn to the front of the wig. Individual hairs are then knotted into this wig lace with a hook, creating the illusion of hair that is growing directly out of the wearer's skin. These wigs look much more realistic. They are also more delicate and must be handled carefully… you should never hold a lace front wig by the lace! A lace front wig can also be a wig that has been made completely from scratch, with all of the hair in the wig being knotted into the lace. These wigs are very lightweight and very natural looking; they are also the most delicate of all the wigs.

Blocking the Wig

Blocking a wig is the act of securing a wig to a wig block with pins before you begin the styling process. Both hard front and lace front wigs must be blocked before you begin working on them. You should never work on a wig that is not properly secured to a wig block—this will cause the wig to slip around on the block or get stretched out of place—possibly even torn.

To block a hard front wig (see Figures 1.17–19):

1. Place the wig block on a wig clamp that is secured to the table.

2. Place the wig on the block. Be sure it is in the proper place on the head—not too far forward or too far back. Check to make sure the side tabs are even.

3. Place a blocking pin in the center front, at each ear tab, and at either side of the nape of the neck. All of these pins should be about one-eighth of an inch from the front of the wig. It is also helpful to place the pins in at a slight angle so that they are less likely to slip out of the wig while you are working.

To block a lace front wig (see Figures 1.20–24):

1. Place the wig block on a wig clamp that is secured to a table.

2. Place the wig on the block, again making sure it is in the right place. Check to make sure that the sides of the hairline are even.

3. Place a blocking pin at either side of the head above each ear, and at either side of the nape of the neck.

4. Use a piece of blocking tape to smooth and hold the lace front in place. The tape should be placed just above the edge of the wig lace. Begin at the center front of the wig and place a blocking pin in the blocking tape. Continue pinning along the hairline, placing a blocking pin every inch or so. Be sure to pin around the hair at the sideburns as well.

5. Secure any loose blocking tape you may have out of the way. This will keep it from getting caught by combs or brushes while you are working.

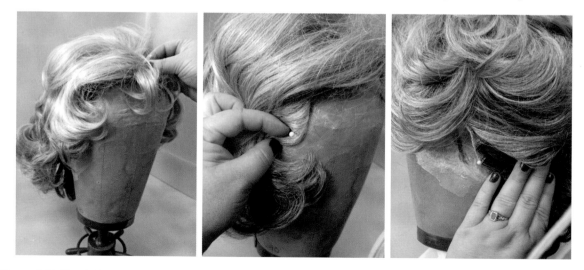

Figures 1.17–19   Blocking a hard front wig: place a pin at the center front hairline (Figure 1.17); at each ear tab (Figure 1.18); and at either side of the nape of the neck (Figure 1.19).

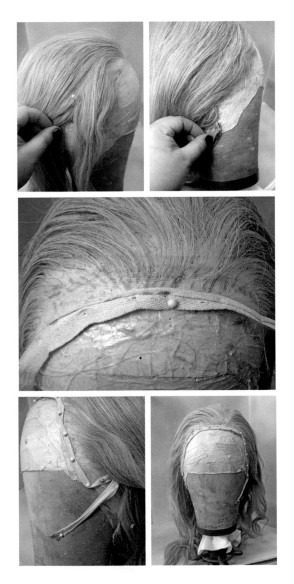

Figures 1.20–24 Blocking a lace front wig. Notice the placement of the blocking pins. Also notice how the tape is secured around the sideburn area (Figure 1.23).

Basic Styling Techniques

Hairstyles are made up of four elements: straight hair, wavy hair, curly hair, and braids/coils/buns. There are a number of ways these different textures can be achieved.

Straight Hair

A human hair wig can be thoroughly wet, combed through and dried to become straight (unless you are working with naturally curly or permed hair). Human hair can also be ironed with a flat iron. To do this, section the hair on the wig into five sections. Begin at the nape of the neck, and run the flat iron through the hair from root to tip. Move from the nape of the neck gradually up to the front hairline of the wig. Work in small sections to get the hair thoroughly straight.

A synthetic wig that is not already straight is straightened by steam. Again, section the wig hair into five sections (the hair should be damp for this). Begin at the nape of the neck. Use a rat tail comb to pull a small section of hair taut. Direct the nozzle of the steamer toward the section of hair at the roots (see Figure 1.25). You should be able to see the hair shaft straighten itself out under the steam. Pull the comb through the hair, moving the steamer along with it until you reach the ends of the hair. Repeat this for every section of the hair, working your way up from the nape of the neck to the front of the hairline. Once the wig is straight, place it in a wig dryer to dry, or allow it to air dry on a shelf.

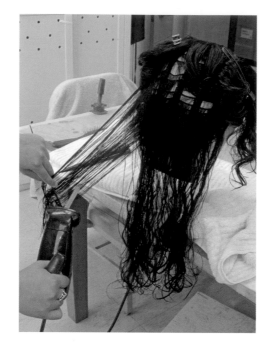

Figure 1.25 Thumper Gosney demonstrates how to properly steam a synthetic wig.

Figure 1.26 Step.1. Thoroughly saturate the hair with setting lotion. Comb the setting lotion through the hair to make sure it gets all the way to the ends.

Wavy Hair

Wavy hair is hair that ripples in an "S" shape. There are three main methods to achieve wavy hair: water waving (also known as finger waving); pin curling; and roller setting. The kind of waves and how much volume you wish for the end product to have will determine which method of waving you choose. All three methods of waving will be demonstrated on one wig.

Water Waving

Water waving, or finger waving, creates a wave that is extremely flat to the head. When combed out, these waves will be larger and softer than those created by the other waving methods. To create water waves:

Figure 1.27 Step 2. Place the part in the wig wherever you wish for it to be. Comb the hair by the part in one direction (either toward or away from the hairline).

Figure 1.28 Step 3. Once you have the hair combed in the direction you want, secure it by pinning a long piece of blocking tape down the center of the wave. The blocking tape will hold the waves in place as you work.

Figure 1.29 Step 4. To create a more defined ridge in the wave, push up with the ribbon before you pin it down.

Figure 1.30 Step 5. The first half of the wave is pinned in place. Pin the ribbon all along the wave.

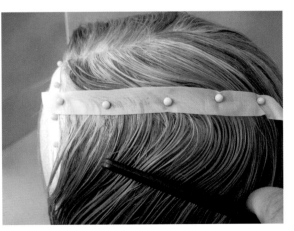

Figure 1.31 Step 6. Next, comb the length of the hair in the opposite direction from the direction you started with.

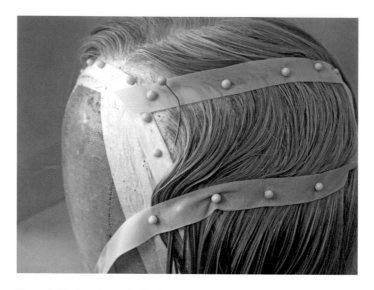

Figure 1.32   Step 7. Use the blocking tape to secure the center of this part of the wave. The first "S" of the wave has been formed.

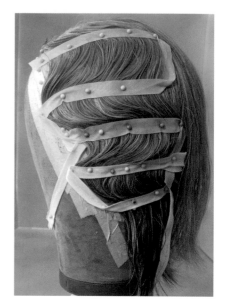

Figure 1.33   Step 8. Continue working your way down the head, alternating directions. You may need to continue to re-wet the hair as you work—it is important that the hair is thoroughly saturated as you are shaping the waves. You can do waves that go all the way around the head, or you can wave a small section of the hair—it all depends on the style you want!

Figure 1.34   Step 9. For a nice finish at the bottom of a water wave, I will often arrange the hair into a pin curl.

Figure 1.35   Step 10. Dry the wig in the wig dryer for at least 75 minutes. When you are ready to comb out the wig, begin by removing the tape. You should start removing the tape at the top of the wig, not the bottom.

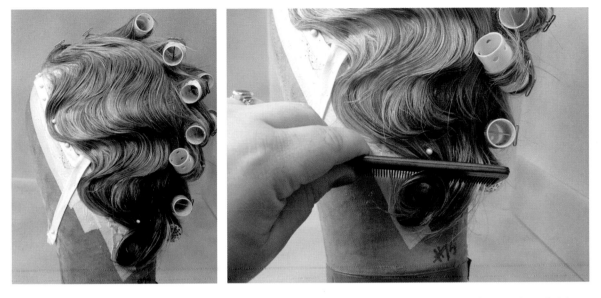

Figure 1.36 Step 11. For a slicker, more shellacked look, you can leave the wig as it is, without combing through the hair.

Figure 1.37 Step 12. If you decide to comb out the waves, begin at the end of the hair and work your way up.

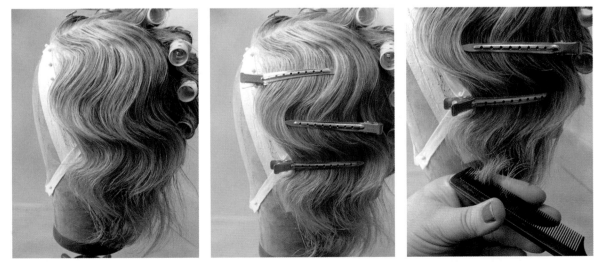

Figure 1.38 Step 13. The combed out wave will be very soft.

Figure 1.39 Step 14. Use duckbill clips to add more definition to the waves, if desired.

Figure 1.40 Step 15. If you wish to neaten the ends of the hair, use a rat tail comb to smooth the ends around your finger.

Once you have completed arranging the waves, mist the wig with hairspray and let it sit overnight. Remove the duckbill clips and the wig should be ready to be worn.

Pin Curling

Pin curling is the traditional method of hair setting that was so popular in the 1930s, 40s, and 50s.

Figure 1.41   Step 1. Again, begin by saturating the hair with setting lotion and combing all of the hair in one direction, starting at the part.

Figure 1.42   Step 2. Use your rat tail comb to separate out a square section of hair, about one inch by one inch.

Figure 1.43   Step 3. Use a dowel rod or other kind of stick to shape your curl and keep it perfectly round. Place an end paper over the ends of the hair, and begin rolling the hair at the tip.

Figure 1.44   Step 4. Once you have wound the hair all the way up to the roots, slide the stick out and secure the curl with pins or clips. (I prefer pins because they do not leave as much of a crimp in the hair.)

Figure 1.45 Step 5. To achieve a perfect wave, the next curls in the row (working down the head from the crown) should go in the same direction. Both of these curls have been wound counterclockwise.

Figure 1.46 Step 6. When you are ready to do the next row, comb all of the hair in the opposite direction from the first row. (In this example, the first row had the hair combed away from the face, so the second row will be combed toward the face.)

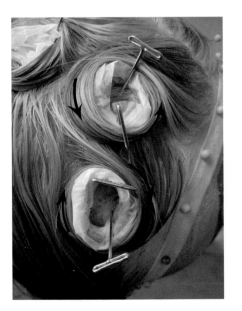

Figure 1.47 Step 7. The next row of pin curls should be wound in the opposite direction as the row above. In this case, the first row was curled counter-clockwise, so the second row is wound clockwise. The arrows indicate the direction.

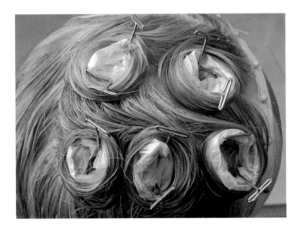

Figure 1.48 Step 8. Continue setting the second row with the pin curls going clockwise. Again, you may need to re-wet the hair as you are working.

Figure 1.49 Step 9. As you work your way down the head, the curl direction will continue to alternate between counter-clockwise and clockwise. When you are done setting the wig, dry it in the wig dryer for at least 75 minutes.

Figure 1.50 Step 10. To comb out the pin curl set, begin by removing the pin curls from the bottom up.

Figure 1.51 Step 11. Use a rat tail comb to comb through all of the curls.

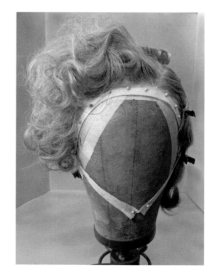

Figure 1.52 Step 12. Notice how much more voluminous the pin curl set is compared to the water wave set.

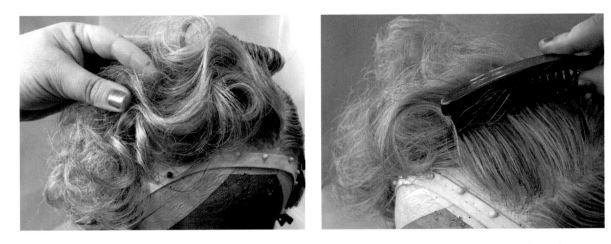

Figure 1.53   Step 13. Begin pinching the waves with your fingers and pushing the hair round until the waves start to fall into place.

Figure 1.54   Step 14. Use a smoothing brush to flatten down the hair and push the waves into place.

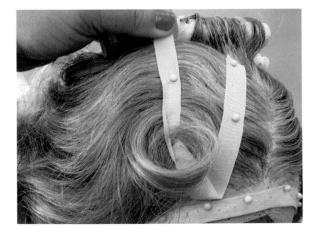

Figure 1.55   Step 15. Pin bias tape in the center of the curve of each section of the wave to set it in place.

Figure 1.56   Step 16. Use the bias tape and your fingers to push up on the wave to make the ridges more defined.

Figure 1.57   Step 17. When you reach the ends of the hair, use the rat tail comb or the smoothing brush to smooth the curls around your fingers. This will create a clean, neat curl.

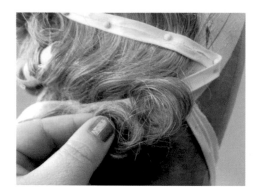

Figure 1.58   Step 18. Slide the finished curl off your finger and arrange it in an attractive way.

Just like with the water wave set, when you are finished arranging the curls you should mist the wig with hairspray and let it sit overnight. Remove the bias tape when you are ready for the wig to be worn.

Roller Setting

Using rollers to set the hair is the most effective way to get a round, neat curl. If you push the curl flat, it becomes a wave. A few notes about roller setting:

Figure 1.59   The section of hair is slightly less wide and deep than the plastic roller.

Figure 1.60   The section of hair should be held taut.

1. The section of hair that you are going to set on the roller should never be wider or deeper than the roller itself.

2. When you are rolling a section of hair, be sure to maintain tension on the hair in order to get a nice smooth set. Letting the hair go slack while the wig is being set will result in a messy wig.

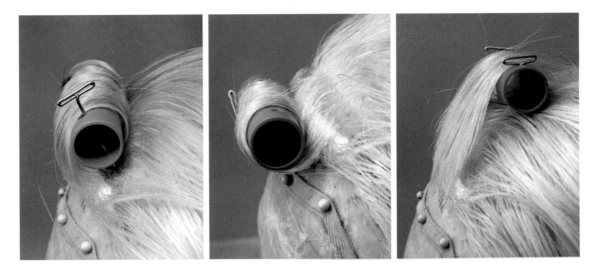

Figures 1.61–63   3. A roller can be set on base (Figure 1.61), forward of base (Figure 1.62), or off base with drag (Figure 1.63). Under most circumstances, you will want to set with the roller on base. For a pompadour effect that adds lots of volume, set the roller forward of base. For a flatter look that sits closer to the head, you may need to set the wig off base with drag.

4. Use a t-pin to secure each roller in place. Turn the t-pin so that it is parallel to the hair in the roller. This will help you avoid snagging hair in the t-pin.

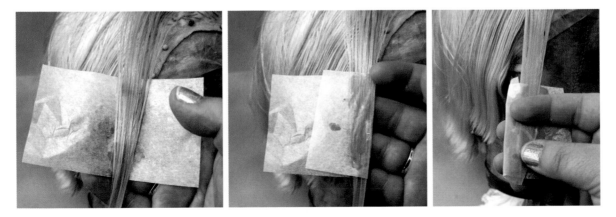

Figures 1.64–66   5. Using an endpaper will give your curls much less frizzy ends. To use an endpaper, slip it behind the section of hair (Figure 1.64), fold each side of the endpaper over toward the center (Figure 1.65), spritz the endpaper with water, and slide it down until the ends of the hair are encased (Figure 1.66). You are new ready to proceed with rolling the section of hair onto a roller.

Roller Setting for Waves

Figure 1.67 Step 1. Begin setting the rollers at the part of the wig. These rollers are to be set off base with a small amount of drag. As you work your way down, make sure that the roller in one row sits over where two rows come together in the next row down. This is called a brick set, because the rollers are offset like bricks in a wall.

Figure 1.68 Step 2. Set the wig from top to bottom.

Figure 1.69 Step 3. Steam the wig if it is synthetic hair and put it in the wig dryer for at least 75 minutes. When you are ready to comb out the set, begin removing the rollers from the bottom.

Figure 1.70 Step 4. After you have removed all of the rollers, you will see gaps in the hair. These are called roller breaks.

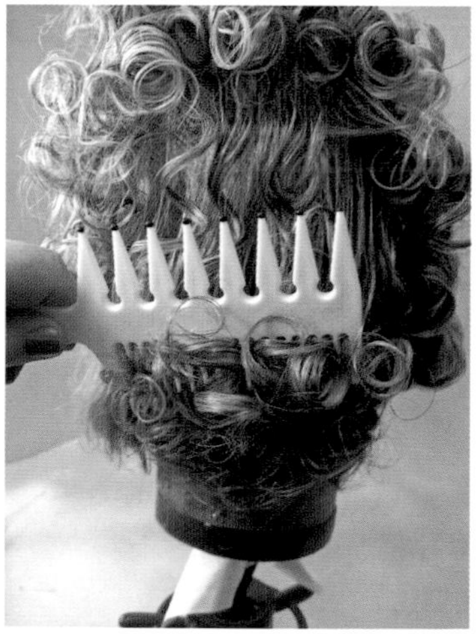

Figure 1.71 Step 5. Use a wide-toothed comb to gently pick through all of the curls. This will help get rid of the roller breaks.

Figure 1.72 Step 6. Run a smoothing brush through the curls to begin shaping the hair into waves.

Figure 1.73 Step 7. Use your fingers to begin pinching and pushing the waves into shape.

Figure 1.74 Step 8. Use a rat tail comb to push the waves in place. Secure them with bias tape.

Figure 1.75 Step 9. Comb the ends of the curls around your fingers to make them smooth and neat.

When you are done, mist the wig with hairspray and let it sit overnight. Remove the bias tape when you are ready for the wig to be worn.

Figures 1.76–78   One wig, set three ways: a water wave set (Figure 1.76), a pin curl set (Figure 1.77), and a roller set (Figure 1.78).

Curly Hair

Just as there are different sizes and shapes of waved hair, there are also different kinds of curly hair. I will now discuss a variety of methods for creating curly hair.

Roller Setting

Hair can be made curly by setting it on rollers, using the same technique as described in the wavy hair section above. The comb out is different, however. Instead of pressing the hair flat into waves, you need to work with the hair in a looser way.

Figure 1.79   Step 1. Unroll the rollers straight out horizontally.

Figure 1.80   Step 2. If you do not brush the curls out, they will be loose and somewhat clumped together.

Figure 1.81   Step 3. Use a large wooden brush to smooth out the curls and get rid of the clumps.

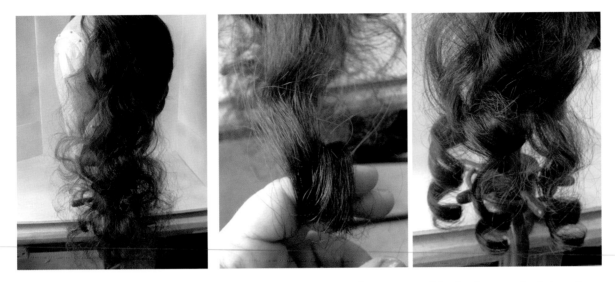

Figure 1.82 Step 4. After brushing, the curls become loose and soft.

Figures 1.83 and 1.84 Step 5. If you want more defined curls, you can brush the ends around your fingers.

Sausage Curls/Ringlets

Sausage curls, or ringlets, are those curls that form a smooth tube of hair. Ideally, there are no gaps in the column of hair. This is a rigid kind of hairstyle that was especially popular in parts of the nineteenth century.

Figure 1.85 Step 1. Separate out a small vertical section of hair and thoroughly wet it.

Figure 1.86 Step 2. Begin rolling the hair around the bottom of the roller.

Figure 1.87 Step 3. As you wind the hair around the roller, make sure you overlap some of the hair every time the hair goes around the roller.

Figure 1.88 Step 4. Pin the roller vertically. Once you have set all of your curls, steam the hair if it is synthetic and dry it in the wig dryer for at least 75 minutes.

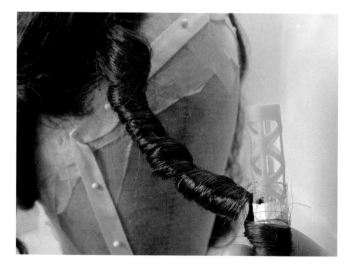

Figure 1.89 Step 5. After the hair is dry, unwind it from the roller.

Figure 1.90 Step 6. You will have a column of hair at this point, but it is usually not as neat and tidy as it could be.

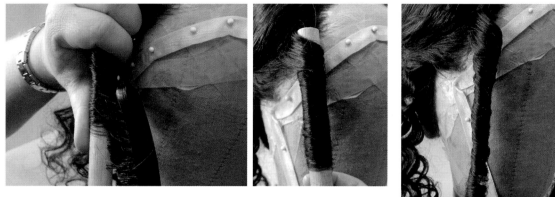

Figure 1.91 and 1.92   Step 7. Use an appropriate size of dowel rod and shape the curl by brushing it around the rod.

Figure 1.93   Step 8. Gently slide the dowel rod out of the bottom of the ringlet. You will be left with a smoother, neater sausage curl.

Spiral Curls

Spiral curls are more a combination of a wave and a curl. This is a very natural-looking curl that is useful for styling many historical looks.

Figure 1.94   Step 1. Again, separate out a vertical section of hair. This section of hair should be of fairly substantial thickness. The size of the section will depend a little on how dense the hair is in your wig, but a section that is at least one inch wide by two inches high is a good starting point. If you make this curl with a section of hair that is too thin, you will end up with a lot of tangled frizz.

Figure 1.95   Step 2. Twist the hair in the direction you want the roller to face. Twist the section of hair tightly, but not so tightly that the hair begins to twist back up on itself.

Figure 1.96   Step 3. Begin rolling the twisted section onto the roller at the bottom.

Figure 1.97   Step 4. As you wind the hair up on the roller, the twisted coils should stack up on top of each other.

Figure 1.98   Step 5. When you reach the top, pin the roller vertically. Steam the hair if necessary and dry it in the wig dryer for 75 minutes.

Figure 1.99   Step 6. Once the hair is dry, unwind it from the roller.

Figure 1.100 Step 7. Notice the snaky look of the hair as it comes off the roller.

Figure 1.101 Step 8. Use your fingers to comb through each section of hair. Each time you comb through the hair, the curls will get softer and less defined. You can also use a wide-toothed comb to comb through the curl.

Figure 1.102 Step 9. The finished curl will be very soft and natural looking.

Curl Clusters

Sometimes, you will discover that you need a cluster of curls in a hairstyle.

Figure 1.103 Step 1. Firmly secure the base of the section where you want it by interlocking two bobby pins. This is done by crossing two bobby pins in an "X" shape. Also make sure that you pin into the base of the wig and not just into the hair itself for a really firm hold.

Figure 1.104 Step 2. Brush the hair around your finger with a smoothing brush.

Figure 1.105 Step 3. Loosely bring the bottom of the curl up toward the base and drape it until it looks pretty.

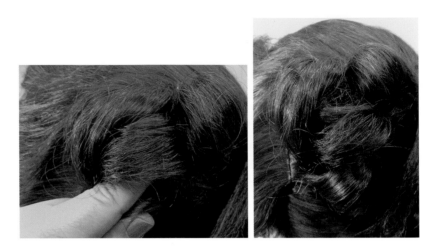

Figures 1.106 and 1.107   Step 4. Secure the arrangement with a couple of bobby pins.

Being able to hide your bobby pins as you work is an important skill. When you are pinning a curl, always place your pins on the inside of a curl (Figure 1.108). When you are pinning a twisted section of hair, insert the pin on the outside of the twist with the bobby pin pointing up (Figure 1.109). Twist the bobby pin up and around into the twist, locking the pin in the inside of the twist (Figure 1.110). Hiding your pins is important whether you are using bobby pins, hair pins, or wig pins. It is also important not to try to pin too much hair at once. If your pin wants to slide back out of a section of hair, it probably means that you are attempting to put too much hair in your pin.

Figures 1.108–110   From left: Figure 1.108—Hiding a bobby pin inside a curl; Figures 1.109 and 1.110—Hiding your bobby pin inside a twist.

Braided Hair

Another commonly used style element is the braid. Braids are a simple, quick way to create a period look.

Traditional Braid

Figure 1.111 Step 1. Separate the section of hair into three strands.

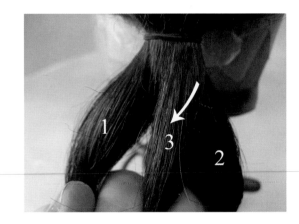

Figure 1.112 Step 2. Cross one of the outside sections over the middle section so that it becomes the new middle section.

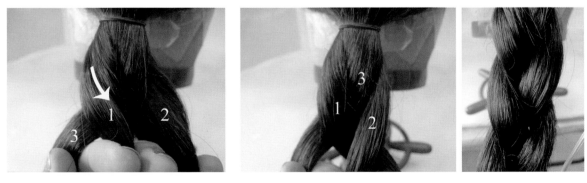

Figure 1.113 Step 3. Cross the other outside section over into the middle.

Figures 1.114 and 1.115 Step 4. Repeat this process until you reach the ends of the hair. Secure the end of the braid with a rubber band or elastic that matches the hair color.

French Braid/Reverse French Braid

A French braid is a braid where not all of the hair is braided at once, and pieces of hair are added into the three sections as you make the braid. This results in a braid that sits very flat to the head and does not create a lot of bulk.

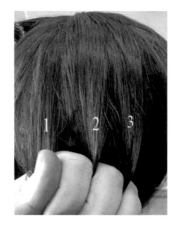

Figure 1.116   Step 1. Separate the hair into three small sections at the top of where you want the braid to begin. The size of the sections will be determined by how intricate you wish the braid to look.

Figure 1.117   Step 2. Braid the hair the same way you did for the traditional braid, crossing the outside sections over to the middle section.

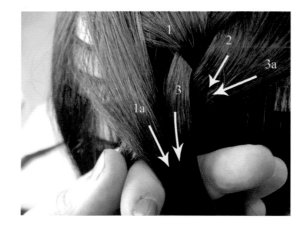

Figure 1.118   Step 3. After making the initial pass through the original hair sections, begin adding more hair to the braid by picking up small sections of hair to add in as you work.

Figure 1.119   Step 4. Continue working your way down the braid, adding sections as you go. The finished braid will sit neatly against the head.

In a reverse French braid (sometimes called a Dutch braid), instead of crossing the section over to the center, you will instead cross them underneath to the center. This will cause the finished braid to look like it is sitting on top of the hair, but still allows the braid to sit very close to the head.

Figure 1.120 Step 1. Again, begin by dividing the hair into three sections.

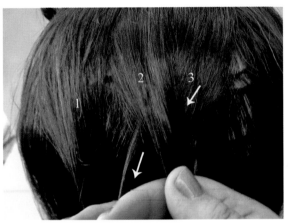

Figure 1.121 Step 2. Cross the outside section under the middle section to begin the braid.

Figure 1.122 Step 3. After you make the initial pass through the first three sections of hair, begin picking up small sections of hair to add into the braid.

Figure 1.123 Step 4. Keep adding sections of hair to the braid until you run out of hair, continuing to cross the sections underneath as you work. Secure the end of the braid with an elastic band. The finished braid will look as though it is sitting on top of the hair.

Rope Braid

A rope braid is a two-strand braid where the sections are twisted together. It is an especially nice braid to use in period hairstyles.

Figure 1.124   Step 1. Separate the hair into two sections. You can either begin with the hair in a ponytail, or with two loose sections of hair.

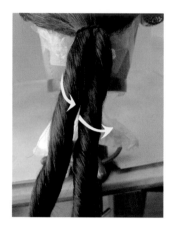

Figure 1.125   Step 2. Twist each section of hair in the same direction. For example, if you twist one section to the right, you must also twist the second section to the right. Do not twist the sections so tightly that they begin to twist back up on themselves.

Figure 1.126   Step 3. Twist the coiled sections of hair together in the opposite direction from the one you did the initial twisting in. For example, if you twisted each section to the right in step 2, you would then twist the two sections together to the left. Secure the end of the braid with an elastic band.

Figure 1.127   Step 4. The finished rope braid.

Fishtail/Herringbone Braid

The fishtail (or herringbone) braid is another braid that begins with two sections of hair. It is another nice braid to use in period hairstyling.

Figure 1.128 Step 1. Divide the hair into two sections. Again, you either start with the hair already in a ponytail, or with two sections of loose hair.

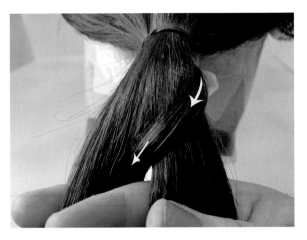

Figure 1.129 Step 2. Take a small section of hair from the outside of one section, and cross it over to the inside of the opposite section. The smaller the section of hair you cross over, the more intricate the finished braid will look.

Figure 1.130 Step 3. Take a section from the outside of the opposite section of hair and cross it over to the inside of the first section. Continue working from side to side until you reach the bottom of the braid. Secure the bottom of the braid with an elastic band.

Figure 1.131 Step 4. The finished fishtail/herringbone braid.

Basic French Twist

One other styling skill that is very useful to know how to do is the basic French twist. Many of the styles in this book incorporate a French twist as a part of the finished style. A French twist is an elegant way to get all of the hair up to the crown of the head.

Figure 1.132   Step 1. Sweep all of the hair in the back of the wig off to one side. Secure the hair with a row of interlocking bobby pins going up the center of the head.

Figure 1.133   Step 2. Gather all of the hair in your hand and twist it.

Figure 1.134   Step 3. Pull the twisted hair up alongside the row of bobby pins.

Figure 1.135   Step 4. Pull the twisted base of the ponytail up over the ponytail.

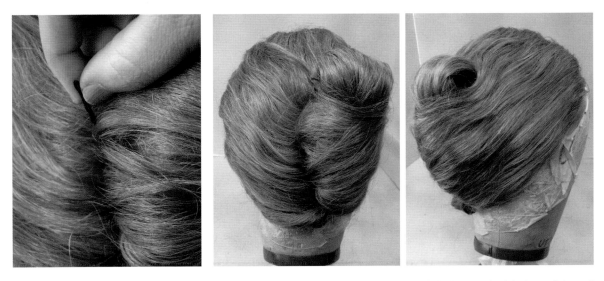

Figure 1.136 Step 5. Secure the roll by tucking and pinning bobby pins all along the roll.

Figures 1.137 and 1.138 Step 6. What you do with the loose ends of the hair will depend on the style you are creating. Here, I simply rolled the ends under to form a curl that completes the French twist.

Using Your Own Hair

All of the styles in this book could be done on a real person's hair if it was the appropriate length. Obviously, you cannot pin rollers directly into a living person's head, but you can recreate the setting pattern with plastic rollers that are allowed to dry overnight or under a bonnet hair dryer (as you might see in a hair salon), with hot rollers, or with a curling iron. Pin curls (secured with clips or hairpins) and braids can also be done on real hair. One thing to keep in mind when styling real hair is that you will need the same supplies readily available to you as you would for styling wigs. If the set illustrated is done with 20 rollers, trying to achieve it with six hot rollers of the wrong size is not realistic. Also keep in mind that many historical hairstyles were either wigs or they incorporated hairpieces. You may also need to use added hairpieces

to achieve the look you are aiming for. These hairpieces would need to be styled in advance of styling the person's hair, using the techniques outlined in this chapter (waving, curling, or braiding.)

Breaking Down/Putting Together a Hairstyle

Once you have mastered all of the basic styling techniques, you must figure out how to put them all together to make a hairstyle. Following the steps for each period in this book will give you a good starting point, but you will want to do variations for each period in order to ensure that you do not create a production full of clones.

The best way to approach putting together a hairstyle is to break the style down into five sections: the front, the left side, the right side, the crown, and the nape. If you examine what each section of hair needs to look like, it becomes much easier to form a plan of attack for the hairstyle. For example, let's look at this detail of a hairstyle from Sandro Botticelli's painting *Primavera* (Figure 1.139). By breaking this style down into sections (Figure 1.140), you can begin to plan how you might style a wig in this hairstyle.

The top/front of the hairstyle (A) is very flat with a center part. The side sections (B) have a tighter, wavier curl. This look could be achieved by setting this section of the hair on dime-sized rollers set in spiral curls. Setting these curls with drag at the roots would help keep section A flat and without much volume. The crown of the wig (C) is also flat, with the ends of the hair going into large, soft curls. There is also a small braid (D) over the crown of the head. At the nape of the neck (E), the large soft curls continue from the crown of the head. These large soft curls in sections C and E could be achieved by setting the hair on quarter-sized rollers, set off base with drag. Figure 1.141 shows a recreation of this hairstyle styled and modeled by Josephine McAdam, where she has added an additional small switch of hair in order to create the braid circling the crown of the head.

Figure 1.139   Botticelli's painting *Primavera*.

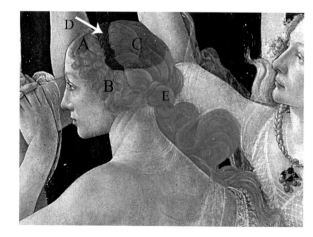

Figure 1.140   The Botticelli hairstyle broken down into sections.

Figure 1.141   Student Josephine McAdam models her version of Botticelli's hairstyle.

Always refer back to your period research and ask yourself, "Is this section of the hair curly?"; "Are there ringlets hanging down in the back?"; "Should the bun be at the crown of the head or at the nape?" and other similar questions in order to figure out the hairstyle.

Hairstyling Tips

Some other tips for putting together a successful hairstyle:

1. Do not try to make your hairstyle too perfect. Wigs look better when they have a slightly more natural look. Humans aren't perfect, and their hair is rarely perfect either. This is not an excuse to style the hair sloppily. Rather, think about putting the style together in a realistic way—real people have hairs that are a bit out of place or not perfectly curled.

2. Have a small bit of the hair break the hairline of the wig somewhere. We rarely see every bit of someone's hairline. Adding little wisps and tendrils helps to both disguise the fact that the hair is a wig and makes the style look more natural.

3. Hairnets are your friend! Use hairnets to secure sections of a hairstyle in place. This will make the section hold better, look neater, and cut down on wig maintenance.

4. The wig will look more natural if it reveals the shape of the skull somewhere. It does not need to be a large section of hair that is plastered down to the head. Rather, even the smallest section of the style that is close to the head will make the wig look more realistic. There are exceptions to this rule—1960s hairstyles, for example, do not generally hug the head anywhere (maybe this is why 60s' hair often looks so wiggy!)

5. Consider the weight and balance of the wig as you style. A wig that is extremely top heavy or back heavy will be uncomfortable for the performer who has to wear it. Also consider whether the wig will need to be worn with a hat or headpiece. Try the hat or headpiece on the wig as you are styling it in order to be sure everything works together.

6. The audience does not wish to see all of the effort that went into styling your wig. Do not overwork the wig so much that it looks like a product-encrusted, tortured wig held together with a hundred carefully placed bobby pins. A proper set and careful hiding of pins will go a long way toward making the hairstyle look graceful.

7. Consider the character. The hair on a character's head says a lot about who they are. It reveals things like social status, environment, and personality. As a wig designer, you can help the actor develop his or her character by making appropriate hair choices. Is the character a buttoned-up librarian whose hair has not moved in 20 years? Is she a social climber whose hair is ridiculously overdone? Is he a Restoration-cra fop who slavishly follows every trend of the day? Make good choices so that the audience knows exactly who the character is.

8. Period is in the silhouette; character is in the details. The overall shape of the hairstyle will let the audience know the period in which the play or film is taking place. The details within that hairstyle determine the character. This includes not only the details of the style itself, but also the details of the hair decorations.

Tips for Using this Book

In each chapter, I have discussed basic looks for each period, including period research. For each major period in fashion history, I have taken you through the steps to create at least one hairstyle representative of that period. Sometimes the style will be a direct copy of a particular reference picture; other styles will be ones I have created by combining several references in order to show you specific techniques. I will note which reference I am working from when applicable. As you become more comfortable with wig styling, you will begin to be able to create different hairstyles based on the basic techniques that are discussed. I have listed in each chapter ideas about variations on these styles. I have also included at the beginning of each chapter a list of artists, designers, and style icons/important people to help get you started on your research into each period.

In the styling examples, I use rollers that are the same size in diameter, but different colors. Different colors do not have any significance in the styling—they just happen to be the colors of the rollers I have. I also do not make any distinction between spring wire rollers or plastic rollers—I use them interchangeably. I will note the size of roller you need to use in order to make the instructions clearer.

For almost every wig style I style, I set a small tendril of hair on a pencil-sized (or smaller) roller in front of the ear (Figure 1.142). I also often (especially when styling an updo) set short tendrils or curls around the nape of the wig, starting back behind the ears (Figure 1.143). These small wispy curls help both hard front wigs and lace front wigs look more realistic by camouflaging the edge of the wig.

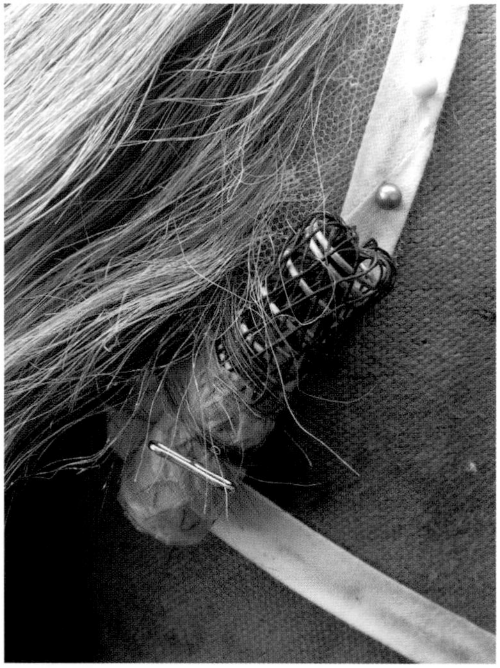

Figure 1.142 A tendril of hair set in front of the ear in the sideburn area of the wig.

Figure 1.143 Tendrils of hair set at the nape of the neck and behind the ears help conceal the back edge of the wig.

For most of the styling examples, I use lace front wigs because they are the ideal choice. If you do not have lace front wigs, you can still create most of the styles in this book. You can adapt wigs in many ways—you can add wefting to them to add volume or length, and you can incorporate hairpieces in order to add to the style of your wig. If you are using a hard front wig, you may need to take extra steps in order to conceal the front edge of the wig. For example, you may need to set additional small tendrils of hair going forward onto the forehead. Other styles have the hair coming onto the face in such a way that the hairline would be covered already. Still other styles are from historical periods where wigs would have been worn, so the wig looking like a wig instead of like natural hair is not an issue. Look carefully at the wigs you have available to you and the style you are trying to create in order to make good choices about what wig will work best for your project.

Practice all of the wig techniques, do a lot of historical period research, and think about your characters. You are now ready to begin creating period hairstyles. The following chapters will guide you through the basics of styling in periods throughout history. Good luck in making many fantastic creations!

two

THE ANCIENT EGYPTIAN ERA

{ *c. 3500 BCE–30 BCE* }

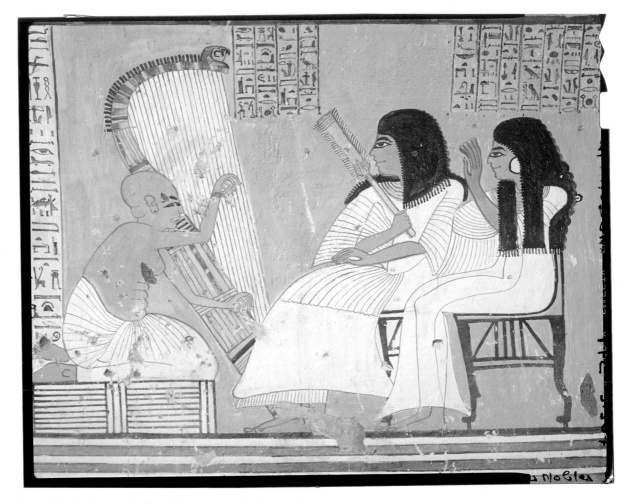

Figure 2.1 The deceased and his wife listening to a blind harpist, from the Tomb of Ankerkhe, Workmen's Tombs, New Kingdom (wall painting), Egyptian 20th Dynasty (1200–1085 BCE) / Valley of the Nobles, Thebes, Egypt / The Bridgeman Art Library.

Ancient Egyptian Women

Ancient Egypt was a great trading city, and as such, was full of racial diversity and worldwide cultural influences. Many people were moving to Egypt from other parts of Africa and Europe. Pictures of Egyptian mummies show that people had a variety of hair colors and textures. The hair colors ranged from dark brown to light golden brown, and the hair textures ranged from Caucasian straight hair to curlier, coarser Afro hair. This racial diversity was very much evident in Egyptian fashion and hair choices. Due to the incredibly warm climate in Egypt, many people simply shaved their heads and wore wigs. In particular, wigs were commonly worn for ceremonial occasions.

Important Events

2600 BCE	Pyramids at Giza built
1400 BCE	Akhenaton drastically changes Egyptian religion
1100 BCE	Upper and Lower Egypt split
332 BCE	Alexander the Great conquers Egypt
196 BCE	The Rosetta Stone is carved
37 BCE	Cleopatra marries Mark Antony
30 BCE	Egypt falls to the Roman Empire

Important People/Style Icons

Ahkenaton, Amenhotep, Cleopatra, Nefertiti (Nefertari), Rameses, Tutankhamun.

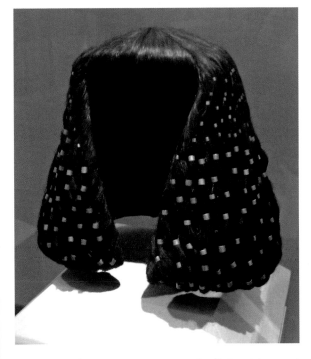

Figure 2.2 A fully intact Egyptian wig, made of hair and decorated with golden bands. This wig is on display at the Metropolitan Museum of Art.

Egyptian wigs could be made out of many different fibers. Some wigs were made of human hair (such as the wig in Figure 2.2); other wigs might be made of wool, and cheaper wigs were actually made of palm fiber. Fancier wigs for important ceremonies might also be made of wood or metal. Egyptian wigs were often heavily ornamented with jewelry, beads, flowers, or ribbons.

Many Egyptian wigs consisted of some arrangement of tight braids or plaits, such as the wigs shown in Figures 2.1 and 2.3.

Figure 2.3 Close-up of an Egyptian alabaster canopic jar depicting the likeness of an Amarna-era Queen, from tomb KV55. Photograph by Keith Schengili-Roberts.

Other Egyptian wigs combined several different textures in order to represent the different racial groups in the country, such as the wig in Figure 2.4. These wigs were often tightly curled on top with tight braids or dreadlocks underneath.

Figure 2.4 This wig, on display in the British Museum, has lighter-colored curly hair on top, and dark-colored plaits on the underlayer.

Yet another kind of Egyptian wig was the tripartite wig, very similar in construction to the full bottom wigs worn in the Restoration period in Europe (see Chapter 9 for more information). Tripartite wigs were divided into three sections—one that sat in front of each shoulder, and one that sat in the back. There is also evidence that false braids and false hair extensions (much like dreadlocks) might have been used to augment a person's natural hair if they chose not to shave their heads.

Late in ancient Egyptian times, the influence of the Romans began to take over. This can be seen especially in the Fayum mummy portraits. These very lifelike paintings were found in mummy tombs. The woman in the portrait in Figure 2.5 wears her hair in an updo that is very Roman in style, but more traditionally African in texture.

Figure 2.5 This Fayum mummy portrait depicts a woman with a ringlet hairstyle, an orange chiton with black bands, and rod-shaped earrings. Currently on display in the Royal Museum of Scotland.

Both men and women in ancient Egypt were very concerned with scent. They would often wear cones of perfumed wax or oil on top of their heads; the wax or oil would melt in the heat and run down the head, cooling it. Extremely high-ranking people might also have vials of perfume built into their wigs.

Ancient Egyptian Men

Like Egyptian women, Egyptian men usually shaved their heads and wore wigs. Their wigs were very similar to those worn by women at this time. Beards were not in fashion in Egypt, but they were considered sacred to the Pharaoh. Pharaohs often wore false plaited beards, such as the one shown in Figure 2.6, on important ceremonial occasions.

on later Egyptian periods, which also explains the growing popularity of beards at that time.

Figure 2.7   A piece of Egyptian artwork depicting a young boy wearing the lock of Horus.

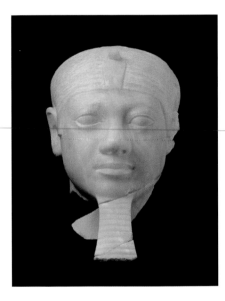

Figure 2.6   Head of King Menkaure (alabaster), found in Menkaura Valley Temple, Giza, Egypt, Old Kingdom, reign of Menkaure, 2532-2510 BCE, Egyptian 4th Dynasty (c. 2613–2498 BCE) / Museum of Fine Arts, Boston, Massachusetts, USA / Harvard University—Museum of Fine Arts Expedition / The Bridgeman Art Library.

Young men often wore their heads shaved except for one long lock of hair that was left unshaved on the right side of the head. This was known as the lock of Horus, as seen in Figure 2.7.

The lock of Horus was ceremonially shaved off when a boy reached the age of 12.

The Fayum mummy portraits also show a range of closely cropped hairstyles worn by men who chose not to shave their heads. These, too, show the Roman influence

Figure 2.8   Fayum mummy portrait of a man with a sword belt, on display at the British Museum.

Ancient Egyptian Woman's Styling—
Step by Step Instructions

For this wig, I used the picture in Figure 2.4 as my main reference.

Figure 2.9   Step 1. Begin with a long hard front wig with some layers (top). The hair should at least 12 inches long at the nape of the neck. For this style, it is often helpful to add some extra weft (bottom) to the wig to make it thicker.

Figure 2.10   Step 2. Sew a row of weft around the inside edge of the wig from the back of one ear to the back of the other ear, stitching all along the nape of the wig. Next, turn the wig right side out and add more rows of weft wherever the wig looks a little thin.

Figure 2.11   Step 3. Trim off the uneven ends so that the wig has a blunt cut in the back.

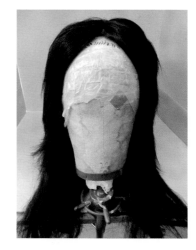

Figure 2.12   Step 4. Part the wig in the center and brush the sides down straight. The wig is now ready to be set.

Figure 2.13   Step 5. Wet the wig with water. Set four pencil-sized rollers on base going straight down from one side of the part. Repeat on the other side.

Figure 2.14   Step 6. Set two rollers in a "V" shape behind the part. Set three more rollers below the "V"; this will connect the two sides in the back.

Figure 2.15   Step 7. Use gradually increasing sizes of rollers to continue setting horizontal rows of curls. The bottom row of rollers should be dime-sized.

Figure 2.16   Step 8. Pin up the bulk of the remaining hair with a clip to get it out of the way. Beginning with the undermost layer, start making a series of tiny braids. Finish each braid with a small rubber band that matches the color of the hair. Braid the remainder of the hair in the wig into small braids.

Ancient Egyptian Woman's Hairstyle—The Finished Set

Figures 2.17–20   The finished Ancient Egyptian Woman's style set.

Once you have finished setting the wig, steam each roller and braid thoroughly if the wig is made of synthetic hair. If the wig is human hair, soak each roller with water sprayed from a spray bottle. After steaming or wetting, place the wig in a wig dryer for 75 minutes.

Figure 2.21 Step 9. Leave the braids in place. Remove all of the rollers from the wig, beginning at the bottom and working your way toward the front hairline. Once all of the rollers have been removed, shape each curl by combing it around your finger. Use duckbill clips to flatten the top of the wig on either side of the part.

Figure 2.22 Step 10. If you want to stretch out the curls so that they hang a little longer, use a curl clip near the end of the curl. This will add weight to the hair and pull the curl straighter.

Figure 2.23 Step 11. The top of the wig should consist of clusters of tight curls. I have added curl clips all along the back to make the curls a little longer.

Figure 2.24 Step 12. Now it is time to add beads to your wig. I used an assorted pack of gold beads purchased at a craft store. I will also incorporate blue and turquoise pony beads purchased from a craft store.

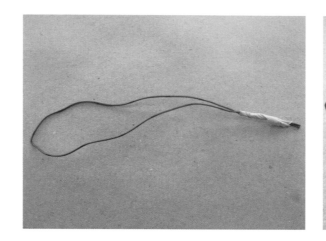

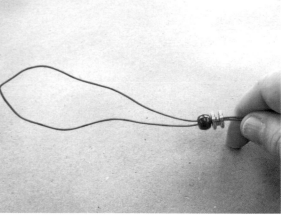

Figure 2.25   Step 13. You will also need a hair beading tool. These are available for sale, but it is easy to make your own. Form a piece of thin wire into a long loop, and bind the end of the wire with masking tape.

Figure 2.26   Step 14. Thread the beads onto the loop the way you want them to sit on the braid.

Figure 2.27   Step 15. Next, thread the end of the braid through the loop above the beads.

Figure 2.28 Step 16. Use the wire loop to pull the hair through the beads.

Figure 2.29 Step 17. Secure the beads by placing a small rubber band underneath them. Slide the beads down so that they catch on the rubber band.

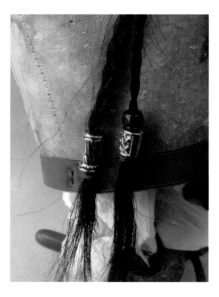

Figure 2.30 Step 18. The finished braid, decorated with beads. You may find that you have to divide your braids into two smaller braids as you work. A braid that is too large might not be able to fit through the holes in the beads. Continue beading all of the braids until you are satisfied with the way the decoration looks.

The Completed Ancient Egyptian Woman's Hairstyle

Figures 2.31–34   The completed Ancient Egyptian Woman's style. Photography: Tim Babiak. Model: Marsherrie Madkins.

Variations

Experiment with different textures of hair in order to create different Egyptian looks. You could use very tightly curled hair on the top of your wig, or you could create more sculptural spirals of hair. You could create a wig entirely of tiny braids, including short braided bangs. You can also vary your looks with the way you decorate the wig.

Use metal and wooden beads to decorate the wig in many different ways. You could even incorporate items such as palm leaves. Other character hairstyles you create may show more of the Roman influences, such as the one shown in Figure 2.5. If all else fails, you can create a shaved head look, à la Nefertiti.

three

THE ANCIENT GREEK ERA

{ c. 2900 BCE–200 BCE }

Figure 3.1   Ladies of the Minoan Court (fresco painting), from the Palace of Knossos, Minoan, c. 1500 BCE / Archaeological Museum of Heraklion, Crete, Greece / Ancient Art and Architecture Collection Ltd. / The Bridgeman Art Library International.

Ancient Greek Women

The golden age of the ancient Greeks lasted for centuries. There were many different ages and periods of Greek history that influenced fashion (among many other things). The Greeks made many important advances in art, philosophy, and science. As Greece was located adjacent to three seas, it served as an important base on trade routes. Greek culture was heavily influenced by other cultures, who brought their customs and fashions through the various Greek ports. Early in Greek civilization, the Minoans were a dominant part of the culture. In Figure 3.1, you can see the women wearing hair with a natural wavy texture that has been dressed with pearls and jeweled bands. This heavy ornamentation of the hair and desirable wavy texture would continue into later Greek periods.

Important Events

1200 BCE	Trojan War is fought
776 BCE	First Olympic Games held
490 BCE	Persian War
468 BCE	Sophocles writes his first tragedy
461–446 BCE	Peloponnesian Wars between Athens and Sparta
336 BCE	Alexander the Great takes the throne of Macedon
200 BCE	First Roman victory over Greece

Important People/Style Icons

The gods and goddesses worshipped by the Ancient Greeks, including Zeus, Hera, Apollo, Aphrodite, Athena, and Artemis; and historical figures such as Alexander the Great, Archimedes, Aspasia, and Helen of Troy.

In the Archaic period of Greek history, many statues called *kore* (maiden) could be found. These statues often featured tightly waved or crimped hair, sometimes accented with elaborate braids (see Figure 3.2).

Figure 3.2 c. 530–55 BCE (marble) (see also 148179), Greek (6th century BCE) / Acropolis Museum, Athens, Greece / Ancient Art and Architecture Collection Ltd. / The Bridgeman Art Library International. Notice the tightly crimped texture of the hairstyle.

Some of these statues represented priestesses; some represented simple female figures. These statues also serve as an example of the Greek love of symmetry. Nearly all Greek hairstyles represented in art are very symmetrical. They usually have a center part, with the hair being waved low across the forehead and then swept back behind the ears. Figure 3.3 is an example of this hairstyle. The hairstyles are nearly always long—short hair was only worn by female slaves or women in mourning.

Figure 3.3   Head of Hera with diadem (marble); Roman copy from the Greek after the "Barberini Hera" type, 5th century BCE. The hair sweeps low across the forehead in a diagonal line towards the ears.

The woman in Figure 3.3 is also wearing a diadem. A diadem was just one kind of hair ornament worn by Ancient Greek women. They might also wear an *ampyx*, or headband. These headbands might be made of metal or leather and were usually worn across the forehead. The most common kind of feminine headdress was the *kekyrphalos*, a type of net or caul that was often made of silk thread or cords and sometimes ornamented with gold.

Figure 3.4   An illustration of a Greek woman's hairstyle featuring both headbands and nets.

Greek women also sometimes bound their hair up with strips of linen. Figure 3.4 illustrates another Greek ideal—the egg or oval shape. This shape was thought to be exceptionally beautiful, and oval shapes are a frequent part of Greek hairstyles.

Figure 3.5　This statue of The Three Kharites (Graces) Dancing in a Circle provides three examples of beautiful, oval-shaped hairstyles. Notice how the hair on the center and right figures continues the diagonal line of the jaw and is piled on the crown of the head, creating an egg shape.

The hairstyles themselves are somewhat simple— the texture, decoration, and shape of the hair often took precedence over the intricacy of the actual style of the hair. The hair was often simply folded or piled and held in place with a decorative ornament. The hairstyles shown in Figure 3.5 are made of simple twists or braids that seem to be held in place with simple linen bands and ornamented with flowers. The ideal hair color for fashionable women was a golden red. Most Mediterranean women had naturally dark hair, so they tried many concoctions for bleaching or coloring their hair to the lighter color they so esteemed.

Ancient Greek Men

Ancient Greek male youths often wore their hair long (sometimes making their hairstyles indistinguishable from women's hairstyles; see Figure 3.6). Once they entered puberty, their hair was cut off in an elaborate, solemn ritual.

Figure 3.7 Diadoumenos' head (bronze), Greek / Ashmolean Museum, University of Oxford, UK / The Bridgeman Art Library International.

worn by Olympic athletes became popular for younger men. As adults, men would often wear a medium-length hairstyle and add a beard to the look to indicate age and wisdom. No matter what the length, a curly or wavy texture was by far the most common look (see Figure 3.8).

Figure 3.6 Apollo of the "Mantua Apollo" type, detail. Marble, Roman copy from the 1st–2nd century BCE after a 5th-century BCE Greek original attributed to Polykleitos. This statue of Apollo features a longer hairstyle. Much like feminine kore hairstyles, the style has a center part pulled back towards the ears, with long wavy hair hanging down.

The shorter hair looks were sometimes ornamented by a headband, such as the one in Figure 3.7.

Boys in Sparta, on the other hand, followed the exact opposite practice: they wore their hair short as children, and then let it grow long once they reached puberty. In the fifth century BCE, the shorter hairstyles

Figure 3.8 A bust of King Philip of Macedon (Alexander the Great's father) with a short- to mid-length curly hairstyle and beard.

Ancient Greek Woman's Styling— Step by Step Instructions

This wig style is based on a combination of Figures 3.2 and 3.5.

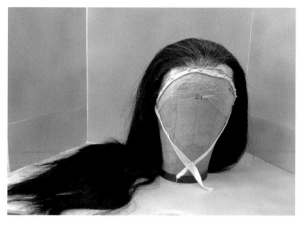

Figure 3.9   Step 1. Begin with a wig that is long (at least 16 inches long at the nape of the neck is ideal) and mostly one length. This wig is a synthetic wig with a lace front.

Figure 3.10   Step 2. Pull a small section of hair in front of the ear and twist it. Set it in a spiral curl. (See Chapter 1 for full instructions on setting spiral curls.)

Figure 3.11   Step 3. Set this curl rolling toward the face in order to create a natural-looking tendril of hair in front of the ear.

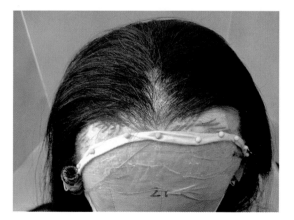

Figure 3.12   Step 4. Part the wig in the center.

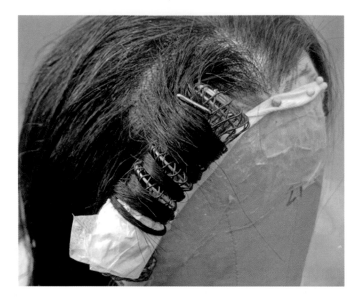

Figure 3.13   Step 5. Take a rather large section of hair (at least two inches by two inches) and twist it toward the face. You will be setting this section of hair into another spiral curl on a nickel-sized roller.

Figure 3.14   Step 6. The finished spiral curl after it has been rolled and pinned.

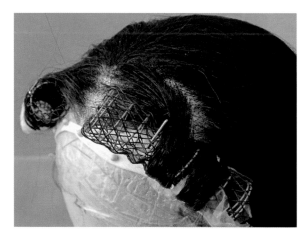

Figure 3.15   Step 7. Roll another spiral curl on the other side of the wig. Be sure to maintain the symmetry of your set and style.

Figure 3.16   Step 8. Move to the next section of hair behind the first curl you set. Twist this section and set another spiral curl going toward the face.

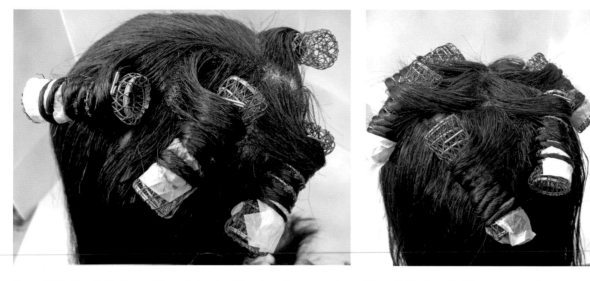

Figure 3.17 Step 9. Continue setting spiral curls until you have three on each side.

Figure 3.18 Step 10. When you get to the center back of the wig, you can set the roller going in either direction.

Figure 3.19 Step 11. Drop down to the next row and set this row of spiral curls going away from the face. Use quarter-sized rollers for this row.

Figure 3.20   Step 12. The finished spiral curl. Notice how the coils of twisted hair stack neatly on top of each other.

Figure 3.21   Step 13. Continue setting a row of spiral curls rolling away from the face. You should have four rollers on each side.

Figure 3.22   Step 14. For the third row of spiral curls, switch back to rolling them toward the face.

Figure 3.23 Step 15. Go back to using nickel-sized rollers for this row of curls.

Figure 3.24 Step 16. Continue setting spiral curls in diagonal rows.

Figure 3.25 Step 17. Finish setting spiral curls at the nape of the wig.

Ancient Greek Woman's Hairstyle—The Finished Set

Figures 3.26–30   The finished Ancient Greek Woman's style set.

Once you have finished setting the wig, steam each curl if the wig is synthetic. If the wig is made of human hair, wet it thoroughly. Place the wig in a wig dryer to dry for at least 75 minutes.

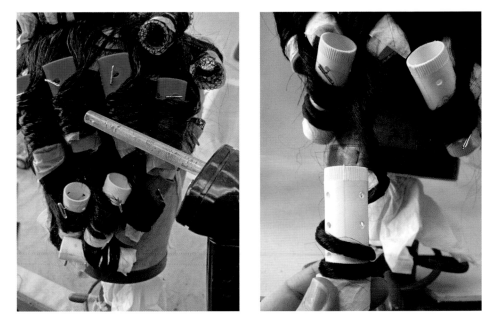

Figure 3.31 Use a small steamer with a nozzle to direct the hair toward each roller. Steam each roller for at least 20 seconds. To style:

Figure 3.32 Step 18. Begin unrolling the set at the nape of the wig. Unwind each of the spiral curls.

Figures 3.33 and 3.34 Step 19. Front and back view of the wig with all of the rollers removed.

Figure 3.35   Step 20. Separate each curl by running your fingers through it like a comb. *Do not use a comb or brush on these curls!* Using a comb or brush will make these curls impossibly frizzy.

Figures 3.36 and 3.37   Step 21. Front and back views of the wig with all curls separated.

Figure 3.38   Step 22. Use a rat tail comb to smooth the first few inches of the hair on top of the wig. This will help you eliminate roller breaks. Do not drag the comb all the way through the length of the hair.

Figure 3.39 Step 23. Take a section of hair from just behind each ear and loosely roll it.

Figure 3.40 Step 24. Pin each roll at the center back of the wig using bobby pins pinned inside the twisted hair.

Figure 3.41 Step 25. Take about half of the hair hanging down in the back and gather it into your hand.

Figure 3.42 Step 26. Loosely fold the hair up toward the crown of the head.

Figure 3.43 Step 27. Pin the center of the fold with bobby pins that are overlapped for stability.

Figure 3.44 Step 28. Pin a hair rat/pad over the bobby pins you just placed.

Figure 3.45 Step 29. Smooth the ends of the folded section of hair back down to cover the hair rat. The remaining loose hair at the nape of the neck should hang down in the back.

Decorate the finished hairstyle with any combination of bands, nets, or metal ornaments that pleases you. I chose to accessorize the wig with golden flora in the front of the wig and a ribbon with a traditional Greek key pattern in the back.

Ancient Greek Woman's Completed Hairstyle

Figures 3.46–49　The completed Ancient Greek Woman's style. Photography: Tim Babiak. Model: Ivy Negron.

Variations

You can vary your Greek styles by choosing to put all of the hair up instead of leaving half hanging down over the back and shoulders.

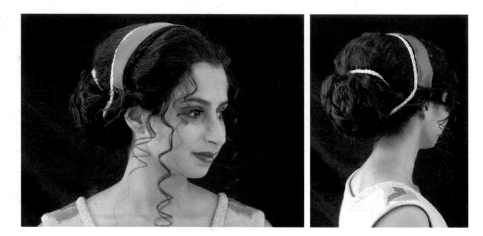

Figures 3.50 and 3.51 All of the hair has been dressed off of the neck in this version of an Ancient Greek style. Wig styled by Thumper Gosney.

You can also incorporate the use of braids into your style.

Figures 3.52 and 3.53 Maur Sela has created a Greek egg-shaped silhouette by using braids in her wig styling.

Again, using creativity and variety in your decorations will help you to create an entire Greek village worth of wig looks.

four

THE ANCIENT ROMAN ERA

{ *c. 600 BCE–476 CE* }

Figure 4.1 Portrait bust (marble) of a Roman woman at the time of Flavius, c. 90 CE, Roma (1st century CE) / Musei Capitolini, Rome, Italy / The Bridgeman Art Library.

Important Events

218 BCE	Hannibal invades Italy
73 BCE	Spartacus leads a slave uprising
45 BCE	Julius Caesar becomes first dictator of Rome
44 BCE	Julius Caesar is assassinated
33 CE	Crucifixion of Jesus Christ
64 CE	Fires destroy much of Rome
305 CE	Constantine becomes the first Christian emperor
410 CE	Visigoths sack Rome

Important People/Style Icons

Agrippina, Julius Caesar, Augustus Caesar, Caligula, Livia, Messalina, Nero.

Ancient Roman Women

The ancient Romans greatly admired the Greeks, and for much of the time of the Roman empire, their fashion choices followed those of the Greeks very closely. Early Roman women's hairstyles were fairly simple. They were often parted in the center, waved or curled, and pulled back into a chignon (see Figure 4.2).

Figure 4.2 Cast of a portrait of Livia Drusilla, wife to Augustus. From the collection of casts of busts showing the members of the Julio-Claudian dynasty. The original artwork is exhibited in the Ny Carlsberg Glyptotek, Copenhagen. Picture by Giovanni Dall'Orto, March 28, 2008. Livia wears her hair simply, in a fashion much like those worn by the Greeks.

Sometimes, a portion of the hair was left hanging down in the back. In Roman society, hair became an easily visible symbol of wealth and status. Hair was often styled by Roman slaves; these skilled hairdressers were known as *ornatrices*. Sometimes these slaves were also required to give up their own hair so that their mistress could wear it. Hair from conquered civilizations was also especially prized as a fashion statement. As curling irons (called *calamistrum*) were developed, Roman hairstyles became more elaborately curled (see Figure 4.3).

Figure 4.4   Marble bust of Matidia, c. 119 CE. This bust shows a Roman woman wearing a diadem in her hair.

Figure 4.3   Head (marble) of Agrippina the Younger (c. 16–59), Roman (1st century CE) / Louvre, Paris, France / Giraudon / The Bridgeman Art Library. Agrippina's hair has been carefully curled around her face with ringlets hanging down in the back.

Roman women began accessorizing their hairstyles with tall diadems worn on the top of the head, an example of which can be seen in Figure 4.4. These hair decorations provided another way for Roman women to display their wealth.

As time progressed, women's hairstyles began to take on the shape of the diadem itself. An example of this hairstyle, which was most popular during the Flavian era, can be seen in Figure 4.1. These hairstyles consisted of elaborately curled hair that was dressed over a metal frame. The back of the hairstyle was pulled into a complicated bun, often with intricate braiding. Wigs were also very popular among the Romans; sometimes wigs were worn right on top of a woman's own hair, as though it were more like a hat than a wig. There were two kinds of Roman wigs: the *galerus*, a half wig or toupee, and the *capillamentum*, a full wig. Blonde hair was believed to be the ideal hair color at this time. This was complicated by a law that required Roman prostitutes to dye their hair yellow! Hair dying was very common among the Romans.

Ancient Roman Men

Early Roman men wore their hair long until professional barbers were introduced around 300 BCE. Short hair then came into fashion.

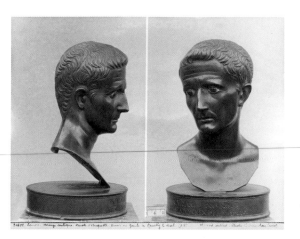

Figure 4.5 Two views of a bust (bronze) of Emperor Augustus (63 BCE–14 CE), Roman (1st century CE), (b/w photo) / Louvre, Paris, France / Giraudon / The Bridgeman Art Library. Augustus wore his hair in a typical short Roman cut that is brushed forward from the crown.

Baldness was considered a deformity by the Romans. Julius Caesar was balding and went to great lengths to try to disguise this fact. He brushed his hair forward from the crown (creating what is now known as the Caesar cut) and he also made wearing a laurel wreath popular (which also helped cover his balding head). Figure 4.5 shows Emperor Augustus wearing a version of the Caesar style. Like Roman women, Roman men also wore wigs and toupees, and sometimes dyed their hair.

Roman men wore their face clean-shaven for quite some time. Short beards later became popular when Hadrian started wearing one. (After all, the Emperor often set the fashions of the day!) An example of a beard from this era can be seen in Figure 4.6.

Figure 4.6 Marble bust of Marcus Aurelius (12–80 CE), Roman (2nd century CE) / Museo Archeologico Nazionale, Naples, Italy / The Bridgeman Art Library.

Ancient Roman Woman's Styling— Step by Step Instructions

For this hairstyle, I used the bust in Figure 4.1 as my primary reference.

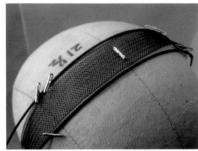

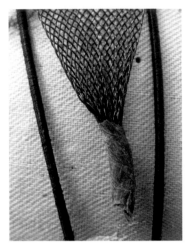

Figure 4.7 Step 1. Before you can begin styling your Roman woman's wig, you will first need to construct a frame to dress the hair over. Begin by laying down a piece of one-inch wide horsehair on top of a canvas block. This will be the base of the headband on top of which you are going to build the frame. Horsehair (also called horsehair braid) is a woven braided strip of plastic fibers that is used to add structure and support to garments. It also has many uses in hat making. It can be purchased at millinery supply stores as well as at some specialty fabric and notions stores.

Figure 4.8 Step 2. Lay down pieces of 18-gauge millinery wire that are about one inch longer than your strip of horsehair on either side of the horsehair. Millinery wire is a fabric wire that is used in hat making. It can be purchased at millinery supply stores.

Figure 4.9 Step 3. Bind off the raw ends of the horsehair by wrapping them with floral tape.

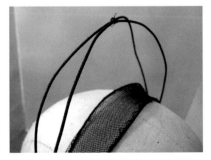

Figure 4.10 Step 4. Use a curved needle to whip stitch the millinery wire to the horsehair, being careful not to stitch it to the canvas block underneath.

Figure 4.11 Step 5. Bend the ends of the wire over with needle-nosed pliers and stitch them in place.

Figure 4.12 Step 6. Place two curved pieces of millinery wire arching up over the headband, going from ear to ear on both the front and back sides of the headband. This wire should rise over the headband by about three inches. If you wish to create a taller frame, you will need to add additional pieces of milliner's wire to support the structure of the frame. Stitch each piece of wire to the ends of the headband you have created. Next, stitch the two pieces of wire together at the center.

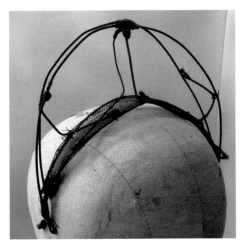

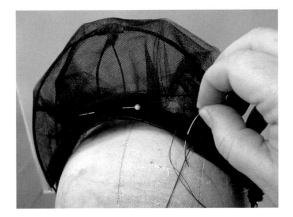

Figure 4.13 Step 7. Take four small pieces of the wire and bend them into an "L" shape. Use these pieces to brace the inside of the frame you are creating. Stitch these pieces to both the headband base and to the tall part of the frame.

Figure 4.14 Step 8. Drape some cheap nylon netting around the frame. Use a color that matches the color of the wig you are styling. This will serve to cover the frame, hold it all together, help to make it opaque, and give you something to pin the hair to while you are styling. Use a curved needle to whip stitch the netting to the wire.

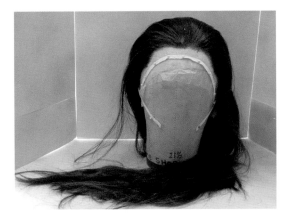

Figure 4.15 Step 9. The completed wig frame, covered in netting.

Figure 4.16 Step 10. You are now ready to set the wig. Begin with a long, mostly one-length wig. A wig that is at least 16 inches long at the nape of the wig is ideal. It is helpful to use a wig that has a lot of hair. If your wig has a lot of visible gaps in the cap, you may need to add in wefting to provide more coverage. I used a synthetic wig with a lace front. This style could also be created with a hard front wig, since many Roman women would have worn a wig anyway; a natural-looking hairline is not a necessity.

Figure 4.17 Step 11. Use pencil-sized rollers to set small curls along the hairline. If you are using a hard front wig you may want to set small perm rod ringlets in front of the hairline of the wig in order to conceal the wig's edge.

Figure 4.18 Step 12. Continue setting small rollers down the side of the face.

Figure 4.19 Step 13. Set a second row of pencil-sized rollers behind the first row.

Figure 4.20 Step 14. Continue setting a third row of rollers that goes in the opposite diagonal direction from the previous row you set. Set a fourth row on dime-sized rollers, again alternating diagonal direction.

Figure 4.21 Step 15. Pull most of the remaining hair into a ponytail at the back of the head. Notice how a fringe of hair all around the outside edge of the wig has been left outside of the ponytail. Braid the ponytail.

Figure 4.22 Step 16. Roll the remaining fringe of hair up toward the ponytail on dime-sized rollers. To create wispy tendrils of hair around the nape of the neck, snip some small pieces of hair and set them on perm rods. This will help to disguise the back edge of the wig.

Ancient Roman Woman's Hairstyle—The Finished Set

Figures 4.23–26 The finished Ancient Roman Woman's style set.

Once you have finished setting the wig, steam each roller thoroughly if the wig is made of synthetic hair. If the wig is human hair, soak each roller with water from a spray bottle. After steaming or wetting, place the wig in a wig dryer for 75 minutes.

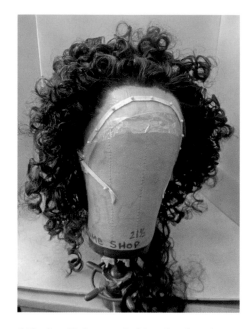

Figure 4.27   Step 17. Remove all of the rollers from the wig. (Leave the braided ponytail in place for now.)

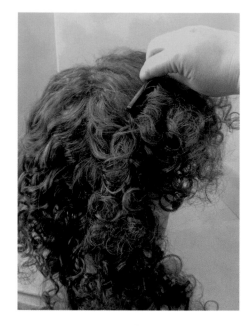

Figure 4.28   Step 18. At the top of the head, comb most of the curly hair forward over the face. Be sure to leave a small section back so that you can cover the wig behind the frame.

Figure 4.29   Step 19. Pin the wire frame in place on top of the head using bobby pins and hairpins.

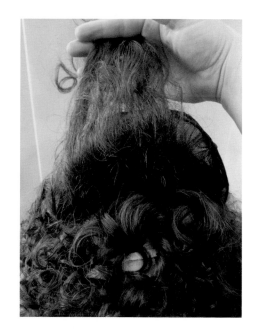

Figure 4.30   Step 20. Take a small amount of hair from the back of the front section of the wig, lightly tease it, and drape it over the frame.

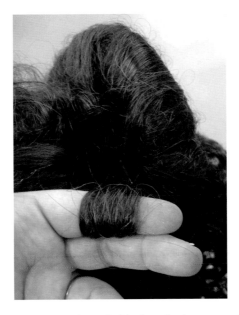

Figure 4.31 Step 21. Pin the draped hair with interlocking bobby pins right at the bottom of the back of the frame. Continue pinning small sections of hair until the frame has been completely covered.

Figure 4.32 Step 22. Once all of the frame has been covered, you will need to form the ends of the hair that you pinned over the frame into curls to cover the back of the frame. To do this, brush each curl around your finger and then pin it in place on the frame with a hairpin until the entire frame is covered with sculpted curls.

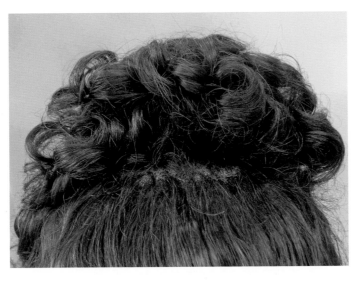

Figure 4.33 Step 23. The back of the frame, once it has been covered with curls.

Figure 4.34 Step 24. Return to the front of the wig and continue forming the hair into ringlets and pinning them to the frame. Notice how enough hair has been left out in the front to do a second row of sculpted curls.

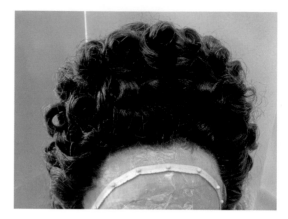

Figure 4.35 Step 25. The completed front ringlet section. Notice how the ends of most of the curls have been pinned so that they form small visible rings of hair. This was done to help the wig look more like the sculptures of this era.

Figure 4.36 Step 26. Unbraid the ponytail, but do not take it down. Gather most of the curled fringe of hair together that you had left behind the frame and make another ponytail directly above the first ponytail you made. Pull the rest of the curled hair (except for the ringlets you have set on perm rods) up from the bottom and add it to the original ponytail. Use a second rubber band right on top of the first one so that you can avoid taking down the ponytail.

Figure 4.37 Step 27. Divide each of the two ponytails into three sections and create three small braids for each ponytail.

Figure 4.38 Step 28. Braid the three braids in each ponytail together to create a very complicated looking braid.

Figure 4.39 Step 29. Wrap the top braided ponytail into a coiled bun and pin it in place with wig pins and bobby pins.

Figure 4.40 Step 30. Wrap the lower braided ponytail around the outside of the bun. Pin it in place with large hairpins. If you need more fullness or coverage in your bun, you can incorporate a braided switch hairpiece into your finished style.

Ancient Roman Woman's Completed Hairstyle

Figures 4.41–44   The completed Ancient Roman Woman's style. Photography: Tim Babiak. Model: Emma Dirks.

Variations

For variety, you can create simpler hairstyles (such as the one in Figure 4.2) with more elaborate jewels and décor creating the silhouette of the period. Decorate these styles with laurel wreaths, cloth and net veils, jeweled nets, and metal diadems. You can pull all of the hair up into the hairstyle, or you can leave some hanging down in the back in a way that references the hairstyles of the Greeks. You can also make use of obviously dyed hair colors in order to make a statement about the status of the character you are creating.

five

THE MEDIEVAL PERIOD
{ *476–13th Century* }

Figure 5.1   Queen Eleanor, 1858 (oil on canvas), Sandys, Anthony Frederick Augustus (1829–1904) / © National Museum Wales / The Bridgeman Art Library. This portrait representation of Queen Eleanor shows a simple maiden's hairstyle.

Important Events

476	Romulus Augustus, the last Roman Emperor in the West, abdicates
800	Charlemagne is crowned as Emperor
1066	The Battle of Hastings is fought
11th, 12th, and 13th Century	European Crusades to the Middle East
1215	The Magna Carta is signed
1250	Chartres Cathedral is completed
1295	Marco Polo publishes his tales of China
1347	Europe is ravaged by the Black Death

Important Artists/Designers

Fra Angelico, Filippo Brunelleschi, Donatello, Lorenzo Ghiberti, Hildegard of Bingen.

Important People/Style Icons

Eleanor of Aquitaine, Blanche of Castile, Henry II, Joan of Arc, King John, Richard the Lionheart, William the Conqueror.

Medieval/Gothic Women

Medieval women's hairstyles were much simpler when compared to the excessive hairstyles of Roman times. Unmarried women often wore their hair loose, wavy, and parted in the center (see Figure 5.2). This wavy texture was often a result of taking the hair out of its customary braids.

Figure 5.2 Eleanor Cross statue (stone), English School (13th century) / Harby, Nottinghamshire, UK / Photo © Neil Holmes / The Bridgeman Art Library. This statue depicts a woman with a center part and a flowing hairstyle.

The length of the hair at this time was still an indication of wealth and status—higher-ranking people had longer hair. High, smooth foreheads were also becoming popular at this time, with some women plucking or shaving their natural hairline in order to achieve the desired look (see Figure 5.3).

Figure 5.3   *The Author Offering his Book to Anne of Brittany*
(1477–1514) from 'Vie des Femmes Célèbres', c. 1505 (vellum)
(detail of 153785), French School (16th century) / Musée Dobrée,
Nantes, France / Giraudon / The Bridgeman Art Library. Notice the
high forehead on the detail of this painting.

Figure 5.4   Detail of illustration from an Italian breviary showing
women's figured silk gowns and a saint / Bilbliothèque Nationale,
Paris, c. 1380. This illustration shows a variety of braided hairstyles
worn by women in the Middle Ages.

The visual interest and detail during this period was
found in both in the braids of this time and on the hats
and headdresses. Women wore their hair in a variety of
braids and plaits, often coiling these around their heads.
The braids might be dressed with decorative cords or
ribbons. Fashion later dictated that married women cover
their heads, so women would cover their hair with a cloth
wimple and place a hat or headdress on top (see Figures
5.4 and 5.5).

Figure 5.5   This medieval statue features elaborately carved braids
as a part of the hairstyle.

Many headdresses were attached to a *barbette*, a cloth band that wound around the head and under the chin, as seen in Figure 5.6.

Another hair fashion that was extremely popular was to wear the hair in coiled braids over each ear. These braids might be covered with an ornamental net or cage called a *crespine* or *crespinette* (see Figure 5.7). This hairstyle was the inspiration for Princess Leia's hairstyle in the *Star Wars* movies.

Figure 5.6   Detail from the Codex Manesse, Ulrich von Singenberg. This woman wears her hair loose with a barbette.

Figure 5.7   Joanna of Bourbon wears a crespine over the braided coils of hair over each of her ears.

Medieval/Gothic Men

Men's hairstyles during the Middle Ages were often dictated by the practicalities of armor and helmets. Men wore their hair in bowl-shaped cuts (see Figure 5.8), sometimes with the back and sides of the head shaved. This allowed their helmets to fit better.

Figure 5.8   Detail of a stern father and two fashionable young men. This illustration shows the bowl cut hairstyle that was popular during the Middle Ages. Also notice the beard depicted on the father.

Men at court might wear a longer version of this hairstyle, known as a pageboy (see Figure 5.9).

Figure 5.9   Portrait of King Richard III (oil on panel), English School (15th century) / Private Collection / The Bridgeman Art Library. King Richard III wears his hair in a pageboy style.

More frivolous courtiers might wear their hair elaborately curled and almost to their shoulders in length (see Figure 5.10). This was especially popular in the Frankish court.

Figure 5.10   Notice the long curled hair of the male courtiers depicted in the Codex Manesse.

Beards became popular for men in the latter part of the Middle Ages (see Figure 5.8). Beards were generally kept neatly groomed, often styled into a point at the chin. Mustaches were not as popular during this time period, and men often wore beards with no mustache at all.

Medieval Maiden Styling—Step by Step Instructions

The hairstyle illustrated here was inspired by a combination of Figures 5.1 (texture) and 5.5 (elaborate braids).

Figure 5.11   Step 1. Begin with the longest possible wig you can find that is all one length (almost waist length is ideal). This particular wig is a synthetic lace front wig that has a section of long bangs, which will be hidden in the finished style.

Figure 5.12   Step 2. Thoroughly soak the wig with water.

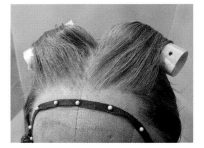

Figure 5.13   Step 3. Part the wig in the center. Set a large spiral curl off base with some drag on either side of the part on quarter-sized rollers. Twist each section of hair before rolling it into a spiral curl. Make sure to use a fairly large section of hair (at least two inches by two inches) for each of these curls so that the end product will be large waves.

Figure 5.14   Step 4. Set another large spiral curl on the crown of the head between the first two curls. Again, use a quarter-sized roller.

Figure 5.15   Step 5. Set the side section of hair in front of each ear in a spiral curl on quarter-sized rollers. Also set a small tendril of hair rolling toward the face in front of each ear.

Figure 5.16   Step 6. Move to the back of the head and divide the remaining hair into three sections. French braid each of these three sections. Using braids to create texture will result in a softer, more natural look than using rollers.

Figure 5.17   Step 7. French braid all three sections of hair in the back of the wig. Secure each braid with a small rubber band.

Medieval Maiden's Hairstyle—The Finished Set

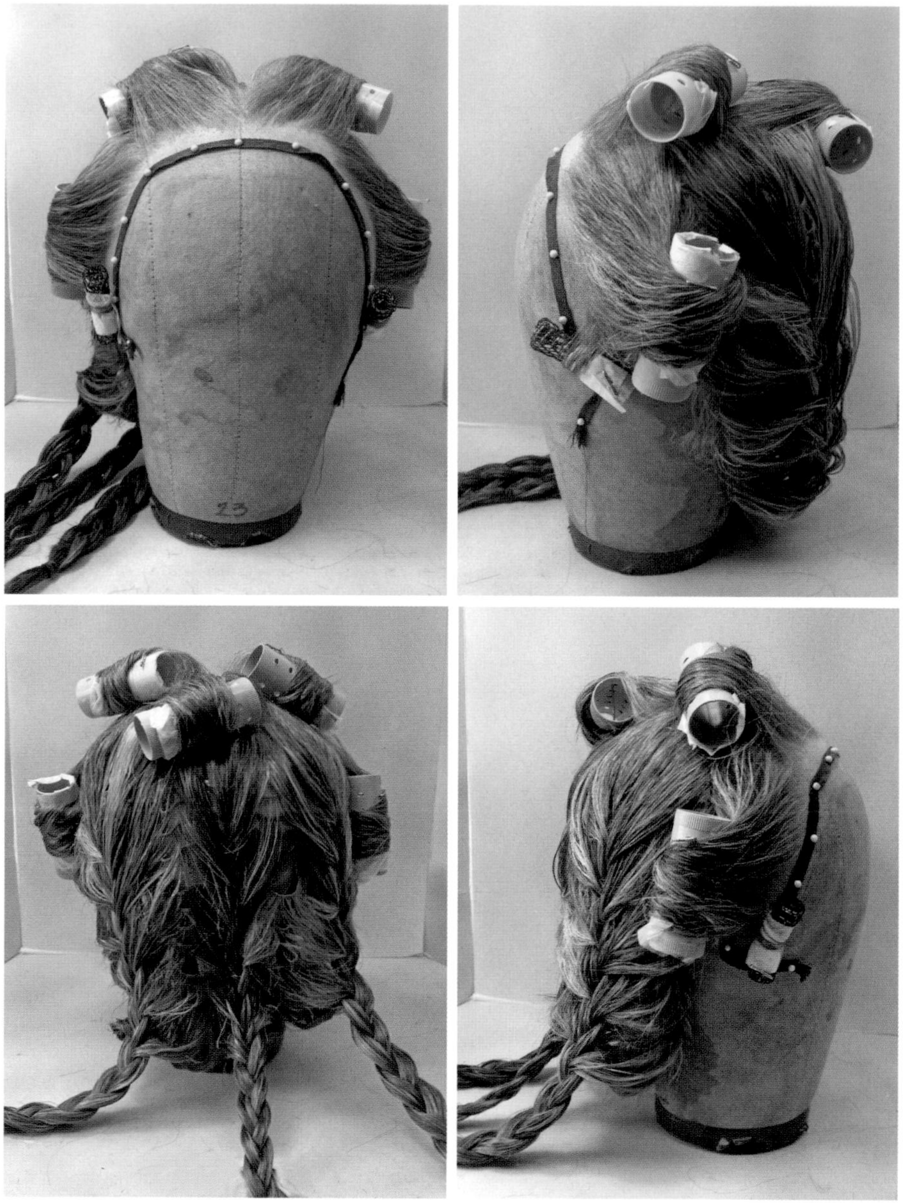

Figures 5.18–21   The finished Medieval Maiden's style set.

Once you have finished setting the wig, steam each roller and braid thoroughly if the wig is made of synthetic hair. If the wig is human hair, soak each roller with water from a spray bottle. After steaming or wetting, place the wig in a wig dryer for 75 minutes.

To style:

Figure 5.22   Step 8. Snip the rubber bands off the braids.

Figure 5.23   Step 9. Undo the braids and remove all of the rollers from the wig.

Figure 5.24   Step 10. Comb through the spiral curls with your fingers in order to break them up into waves.

Figure 5.25   Step 11. Comb through the entire wig with a wide-toothed comb.

Figure 5.26   Step 12. Use a teasing/smoothing brush to brush through the first few inches of the front section of the wig. Do not brush all the way through to the ends of the hair; rather, just use the brush to break up any remaining roller breaks at the roots.

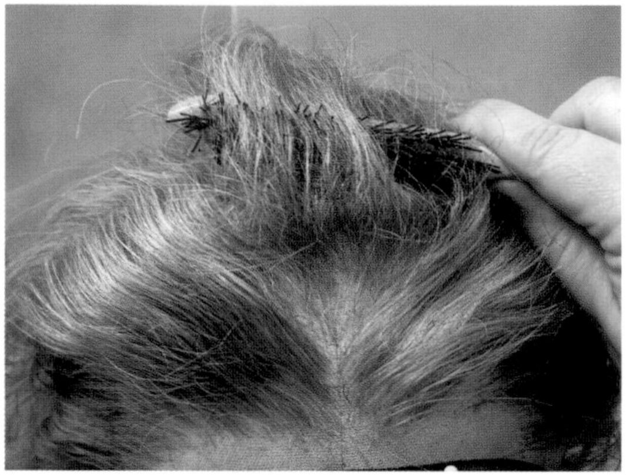

Figure 5.27   Step 13. Use a teasing/smoothing brush to lightly tease the section of hair right behind the center part.

Figure 5.28   Step 14. Pick up a section of hair at the side of the head and divide it into three sections with your fingers. You are going to braid this section into a reverse French braid (the braid should come out on top as you braid—see Chapter 1 for more detailed instructions).

Figure 5.29   Step 15. Begin the reverse French braid moving horizontally along the head. As you work, only pick up and add hair from above/on top of the head. Do not add in any hair from below the braid.

Figure 5.30   Step 16. Once you reach the center of the head, braid the rest of the hair you are holding in your hand. Braid this hair in a regular braid, not a French braid. Tie off the bottom of the braid with a small rubber band.

Figure 5.31   Step 17. Braid the other side of the wig in the same manner so that the sides mirror each other.

Figure 5.32   Step 18. Wrap one braid around the head in a circular shape, pinning it with bobby pins as you go.

Figures 5.33 and 5.34   Step 19. Wrap the other braid up around the crown of the head in the opposite direction from the first braid. Tuck your ends in underneath the other braid. Use bobby pins to pin both braids in place.

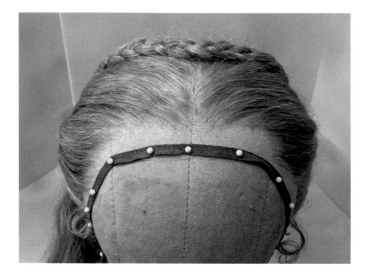

Figure 5.35   Step 20. From the front of the wig, the circle of braids should just be visible.

Figure 5.36   Step 21. Take a small section of hair just behind each ear and braid it into a fishtail/herringbone braid (see Chapter 1 for instructions).

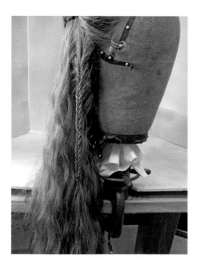

Figure 5.37   Step 22. Bind off these braids a few inches up from the bottom.

Figure 5.38   Step 23. Thread ribbons into the braids to add decoration to the wig. The ribbons could be braided into the hair from the beginning, but I prefer to use a blunt sewing needle with a large eye so that I have more control over the ribbon placement. I thread the ribbon through the needle, and then weave the threaded ribbon in and out of the braid until it looks the way I want.

Medieval Maiden—The Completed Hairstyle

Figures 5.39–42   The completed Medieval Maiden's style. Photography: Tim Babiak. Model: Josephine McAdam.

Variations

You can configure the braids in this wig to create a wide variation of styles for the medieval period. For example, you could braid all of the hair in the wig instead of leaving the back section hanging down. Once braided, you could either wrap the braid around the head or leave it hanging down the back. You can create more interesting braids by either twisting two regular braids together, or by braiding three small braids together. This will give you a braid that looks incredibly complicated, but is actually fairly easy to achieve.

You can also create hairstyles with a curlier texture of hair for this era. You can also use crowns, ribbons, nets, and cages to add variety to the décor of these hairstyles.

Figure 5.44   This medieval statue shows a woman with hair that has a very curly texture.

Figure 5.43   Two regular braids have been twisted together in order to form one more intricate-looking braid.

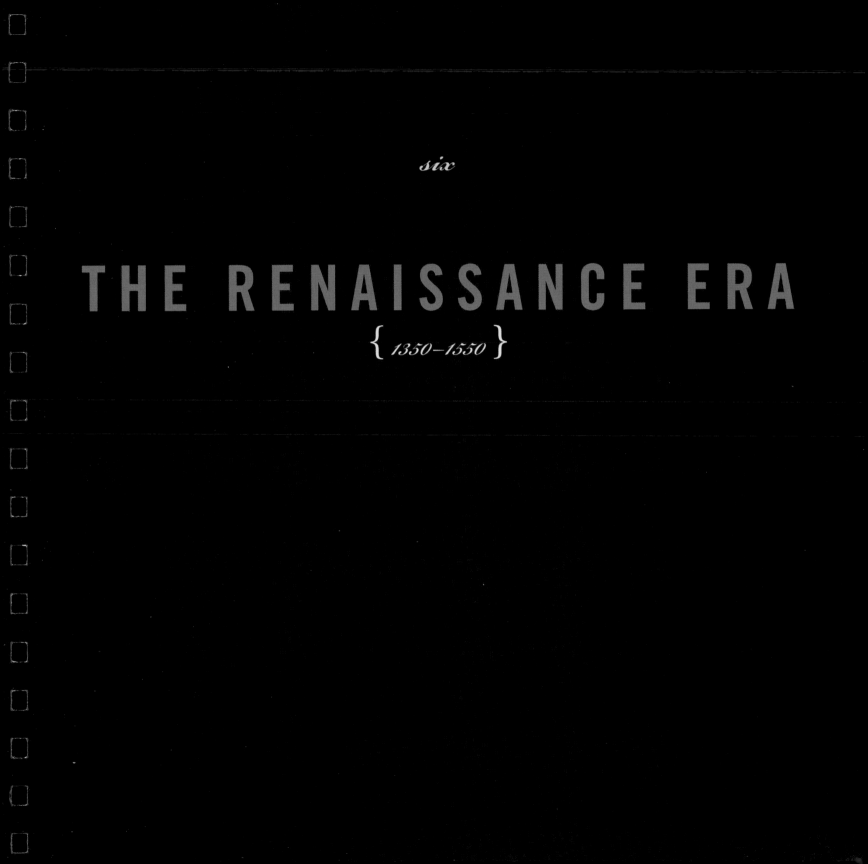

six

THE RENAISSANCE ERA

{ *1350–1550* }

Figure 6.1 *Portrait of a Young Woman*, 1485 (tempera on panel), Botticelli, Sandro (1444/5–1510) / Stadelsches Kunstinstitut, Frankfurt-am-Main, Germany / The Bridgeman Art Library International.

Important Events

Important Artists/Designers

Sandro Botticelli, Leonardo da Vinci, Albrecht Dürer, Jan van Eyck, Hans Holbein, Michelangelo, Raphael, Titian.

Important People/Style Icons

Anne Boleyn, Anne of Cleves, Catherine of Aragon, the de Medici family, Diane de Poitiers, Ferdinand and Isabella of Spain, Henry VIII, Catherine Howard, Katherine Parr.

Renaissance Women

The Renaissance was a cultural movement and a time of great learning, invention, and enlightenment. This movement began in Italy in the 1300s and gradually spread throughout Europe. Fashion and luxury went hand in hand during this period—fine fabrics and furs became more available and highly sought after. Hairstyles, when uncovered, were just as elaborate and highly trimmed and ornamented as clothing. For women of the Renaissance period, the focus of fashion was still to elaborately dress the hair with nets, cauls, wimples, caps, and headdresses. High foreheads were still in fashion, with many women plucking back their hairline so that their foreheads appeared higher (see Figure 6.2).

Figure 6.2   *Portrait of a Lady in Red*, 1460–70 (oil and tempera on panel), Italian School, (15th century) / National Gallery, London, UK / Giraudon / The Bridgeman Art Library International. This portrait is an example of both the Renaissance high forehead and the elaborate nets used to dress hair at the time.

Light hair colors remained popular, such as the red hair seen in Figure 6.1, and the golden hair seen in Figure 6.2. Married women, when their hair was not covered by elaborate headdresses, wore their hair in elaborate updos. These hairstyles usually had clearly divided sections—there was a center part; the side front sections had a curly or wavy texture; and the back was an elaborate arrangement of braids and coils (see Figure 6.3).

Figure 6.4   Head of a young girl in profile to the left in Renaissance dress (pen and brown ink and bodycolour on vellum), German School (19th century) / Private Collection / Photo © Christie's Images / The Bridgeman Art Library International. This young girl wears a braid covered by crossed ribbons.

Figure 6.3   Giovanna Tornabuoni, née Albizzi, 1488, detail (oil on panel), Ghirlandaio, Domenico (Domenico Bigordi) (1449–94) / Thyssen-Bornemisza Collection, Madrid, Spain / The Bridgeman Art Library International. Notice the clearly divided sections of the hairstyle in this portrait—some sections of the hair are very smooth, and some have a defined wavy texture.

Young, unmarried women had more freedom to wear their hair down or loose. When hair was allowed to hang down, it was sometimes tightly braided (see Figure 6.4). The braids were also accented with pearls, ribbons, cords, and net.

Sometimes the hair was allowed to hang loose without being braided, such as in Figure 6.1. The loose hair often had a wavy texture, which could have either been the hair's natural texture, or texture resulting from being braided for long periods of time.

Because the hairstyles of this time were so intricate, false hair was often needed in order to achieve these looks. Hair was also sometimes dressed over an understructure, such as the *balzo*. The *balzo* was a bulbous shaped frame that bulged out over the back of the head, and was covered with false hair.

Renaissance Men

Hats were just as important for men as they were for women in the Renaissance. These hats were often flat and soft on top. For young men, long flowing locks were very popular. The length of hair could be anywhere between the chin and the shoulders, and usually had a wavy texture (see Figure 6.5).

Figure 6.6 *Self Portrait with a Thistle*, 1493 (oil on vellum), Dürer, Albrecht (1471–1528) / Louvre, Paris, France / The Bridgeman Art Library International. Dürer wears the longer hair and clean-shaven face typical of young Renaissance men.

Older men generally wore their hair shorter. They were also more likely to wear beards, such as the one made popular by King Henry VIII of England (see Figure 6.7).

Figure 6.5 Portrait of a young man holding a medallion of Cosimo I de Medici ('The Elder') (1389–1463) (tempera on panel) (see BEN44369), Botticelli, Sandro (1444/5–1510) / Galleria degli Uffizi, Florence, Italy / Alinari / The Bridgeman Art Library International. This young man wears his hair long and wavy under a cap.

These hairstyles either had bangs (as in Figure 6.5) or were swept away from the forehead (as in Figure 6.6). Young men of this time were usually clean-shaven.

Figure 6.7 Portrait of Henry VIII, 1491–1547 (tempera on wood), Hans Holbein the Younger, c. 1539–40 / Galleria Nazionale d'Arte Antica. Henry VIII wears shorter hair and a square beard.

Renaissance Woman's Styling—Step by Step Instrctions

The inspiration for this hairstyle is a combination of Figures 6.1 and 6.3. I wanted to incorporate the long wavy texture seen in Figure 6.1, and the coiled braids seen in Figure 6.3.

Figure 6.8   Step 1. Begin with a wig that is thick, dense, and long—preferably at least 16 inches long at the nape of the neck. Short layers around the face can be useful for this look as well. You will also need a switch (ponytail) of hair in a matching hair color. I used a synthetic lace front wig. You could also achieve this look with a shoulder length wig that has one or two switches incorporated into the final hairstyle.

Figures 6.9 and 6.10   Step 2. Section the hair into four sections: front left, front right, crown of the head, and nape of the neck.

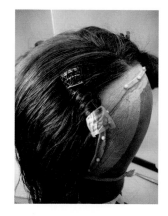

Figure 6.11   Step 3. Make a center part in the front of the wig. Leave a couple of inches of straight hair, and then set a curl going away from the face on a dime-sized roller.

Figure 6.12   Step 4. Set two more curls on the top row on dime-sized rollers. Also set the row below on dime-sized rollers, but roll these curls toward the face. Repeat on the other side of the head.

Figure 6.13 Step 5. Pull the crown section of hair into a ponytail. Make two small rope braids on either side of the ponytail, leaving the center of the ponytail loose.

Figure 6.14 Step 6. Set the rest of the hair in the ponytail on nickel-sized rollers.

Figures 6.15 and 6.16 Step 7. Set the bottom section of hair on nickel-sized rollers. Set this hair using the spiral rolling technique discussed in Chapter 1, making sure to twist each section of hair before rolling it.

Renaissance Woman's Hairstyle—The Finished Set

Figures 6.17–20   The finished Renaissance Woman's style set.

Once you have finished setting the wig, steam each roller thoroughly if the wig is made of synthetic hair. If the wig is human hair, soak each roller with water sprayed from a spray bottle. After steaming or wetting, place the wig in a wig dryer for 75 minutes.

To style:

Figure 6.21   Step 8. Begin removing the rollers at the bottom of the wig until all the rollers have been removed.

Figure 6.22   Step 9. Use a wide-toothed comb to comb through the front two sections of hair.

Figure 6.23   Step 10. Use a smoothing brush to shape the front curls around your finger. Do this for all of the hair in the front sections.

Figure 6.24   Step 11. Take a small section of hair from the bottom of each side of the front sections of hair.

Figure 6.25   Step 12. Smooth these back and bobby pin them right next to the ponytail.

Figure 6.26 Step 13. Brush through all of the hair in the ponytail except for the two rope braids. Include the two side sections in this hair. Roll up a hair rat with this hair, forming a bun.

Figure 6.27 Step 14. Pin the bun in place and smooth any flyaway hairs. You may wish to put a hairnet over this bun. Hairnets can be very useful for holding all the parts of a bun securely in place. They also help smooth down flyaway hairs. They are especially handy when you are incorporating hairpieces into your style—they help hold all of the parts together.

Figure 6.28 Step 15. Pin the matching switch of hair into the base of the ponytail with bobby pins.

Figure 6.29 Step 16. Form the switch into a rope braid. Wrap the rope braid around the bun, pinning it with large hairpins as you work your way around the bun.

Figure 6.30 Step 17. Tuck the end of the switch under and pin it in a way that looks good and is very secure.

Figure 6.31 Step 18. Use a tiny rubber band to secure a string of pearls to one of the rope braids. Wrap the pearls around the braid and secure them at the bottom with another rubber band. Repeat with the other small rope braid.

Figure 6.32 Step 19. Wrap one small rope braid across the center of the bun. Wrap the second braid around the outside of the bun. Pin both braids in place with bobby pins.

Figure 6.33 Step 20. Use your fingers to comb through the spiral curls at the nape of the wig.

Figure 6.34 Step 21. Use blocking tape to shape the waves in the front of the wig. Mist these with hairspray and let them set overnight.

Renaissance Woman—The Finished Hairstyle

Figures 6.35–38 The completed Renaissance Woman's style. Photography: Tim Babiak. Model: Sabrina Lotfi.

Variations

Renaissance women's hairstyles are so elaborate that it is easy to create variety. There are endless ways to arrange braids, add decoration, and configure the different sections of hair. You can also choose to put the majority of the hair up, or leave it hanging down.

There is also great room for playing with texture in Renaissance wigs. Using some sections that have a lot of texture and some where the texture is smooth creates a nice study in contrasts.

Figure 6.39   This hairstyle, styled by Thumper Gosney, has had most of the hair put up, with only a few tendrils hanging down. Also note the elaborate arrangement of braids. Model: Juliet Robb.

Figure 6.40   This wig, styled and modeled by Chelsea Bunn, is an example of an interesting use of textures. The hair accessory worn here would also be very useful for hiding the front edge of a hard front wig.

Renaissance Man's Styling—Step by Step Instructions

This hairstyle is a combination of the styles seen in Figures 6.5 and 6.6.

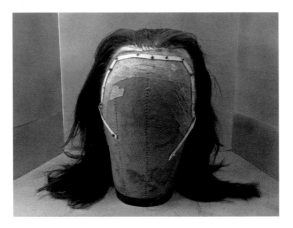

Figure 6.41   Step 1. Begin with a wig that is between chin and shoulder length on your performer. A layered wig would also work with this style. I used a synthetic hair lace front wig.

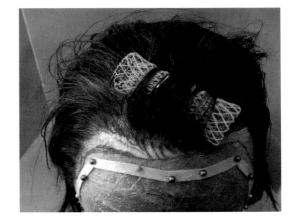

Figure 6.42   Step 2. Use a nickel-sized roller to set the first curl at a slight angle to the front hairline. This will add a natural looking wave to the finished style. Set two more nickel-sized rollers behind the first roller.

Figure 6.43   Step 3. Use a dowel rod to shape a pin curl on the side of the head. Use a large, square section of hair for the pin curl—at least two inches by two inches. The pin curl has been set going counterclockwise. Setting the hair with a pin curl instead of a roller creates less volume in the finished product. Men's wigs look much more realistic if they do not have a lot of volume.

Figure 6.44   Step 4. Use the dowel rod to form a second pin curl directly below the first one. Create two more pin curls on the opposite side of the wig.

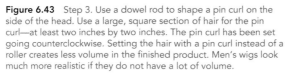

Figure 6.45   Step 5. Continue using the dowel rod to form a row of counter-clockwise pin curls going across the crown of the wig.

Figure 6.46   Step 6. Form a second row of clockwise pin curls below the first row of pin curls. Notice how much drag there is at the roots of the hair. This flat hair will help keep the volume out of your wig.

Figure 6.47   Step 7. The rest of the wig will be set in spiral curls. Twist each section before the setting the spiral curl on a nickel-sized roller.

Figure 6.48   Step 8. The remainder of the hair at the nape of the wig should be set in spiral curls going in alternating diagonal rows. Make sure to twist each section of hair before rolling it.

Renaissance Man's Hairstyle—The Finished Set

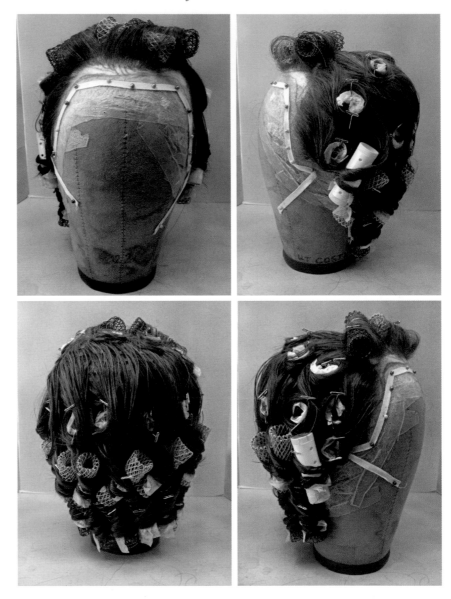

Figures 6.49–52   The finished Renaissance Man's style set.

Once you have finished setting the wig, steam each roller thoroughly if the wig is made of synthetic hair. If the wig is human hair, soak each roller with water from a spray bottle. After steaming or wetting, place the wig in a wig dryer for 75 minutes.

To style:

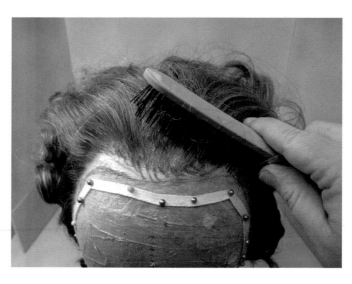

Figure 6.53 Step 9. Remove all of the rollers from the wig, beginning at the nape of the neck and working your way up toward the front hairline.

Figure 6.54 Step 10. Use a teasing/smoothing brush to brush through the top front section of the wig. Use the brush to push a wave into this section of hair.

Figure 6.55 Step 11. Use a wide-toothed comb to comb through the rest of the wig.

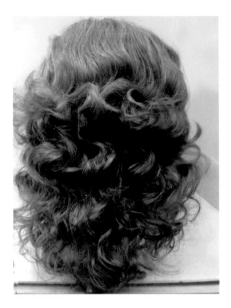

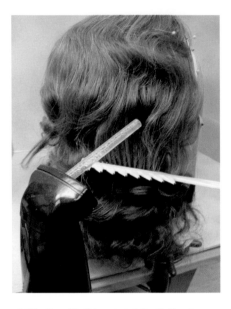

Figure 6.56   Step 12. Once the wig has been combed out, you should have soft, natural-looking waves. This look is similar to the hair in Figure 6.5.

Figure 6.57   Step 13. If the wig is fuller/fluffier than you want it to be, quickly pass a steamer over the section you want to be flatter and comb through it so that the waves loosen. (If you are using a human hair wig, very lightly mist the wig with water and comb through it to achieve the same effect.)

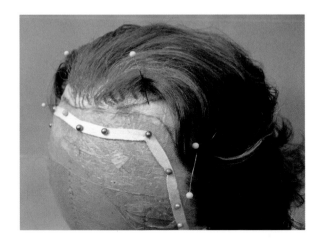

Figure 6.58   Step 14. Use blocking pins to shape the hair around the face. Mist this hair with hairspray and let it set overnight. It is especially helpful on men's wigs to have a section of hair that dips down a little bit onto the face. This helps make the hairstyle look more realistic.

Renaissance Man—The Completed Hairstyle

Figures 6.59–62   The completed Renaissance Man's style. Photography: Tim Babiak. Model: Leslie Hethcox.

Variations

Just as with Renaissance women's styles, you can create variety in your Renaissance men's styles by varying the texture of the hair. Make some styles fluffier and curlier; others could be straighter or wavier. Include a variety of hair lengths from right at the chin to past the shoulders. Consider using hats to further differentiate your characters.

seven

THE ELIZABETHAN ERA

{ *1500–1603* }

Figure 7.1   Portrait of Queen Elizabeth I – The Armada Portrait (oil on canvas), Gower, George (1540–96) (manner of) / Private Collection / Photo © Philip Mould Ltd, London / The Bridgeman Art Library International.

Important Events

1536	Michelangelo begins to paint *The Last Judgment* in the Sistine Chapel
1543	Mary is crowned Queen of Scots
1547	Henry VIII dies
1553	Lady Jane Grey is queen for nine days
1556	Thomas Cranmer, former Archbishop of Canterbury, is burned at the stake
1558	Elizabeth I becomes Queen of England
1588	England defeats the Spanish Armada
1603	Queen Elizabeth I dies

Important Artists

Nicholas Hilliard, Hans Holbein the Younger, George Gower, Marcus Gheeraerts II, Steven van der Muelen, Titian, Agnolo Bronzino, Michelangelo Merisi da Caravaggio.

Important People/Style Icons

Queen Elizabeth I, Mary Queen of Scots, Lady Jane Grey, Sir Walter Raleigh, William Shakespeare, Sir Francis Drake, Robert Dudley, Sir Francis Bacon.

Elizabethan Women

The Elizabethan era is also often referred to as the Peacock Age. Queen Elizabeth I of England set the ideal of feminine fashion for this time—among her many accoutrements, she was rumored to have more than 80 wigs. This is just one example of the excess in fashion and décor seen during this period. Elizabeth's fondness for red hair, white skin, and red lips and cheeks had many courtiers of the time imitating her in the hopes of winning her favor. The red hair dyes used during this period were quite caustic and often caused women's hairlines to recede slightly.

Figure 7.2 *Portrait of a Lady* (oil on panel), Clouet, Francois (c. 1510–72) / Private Collection / The Bridgeman Art Library International. Notice both the heart shape of this hairstyle and how the lady's ruff practically forces the hair to be off of her neck.

Blonde hair was also still in vogue and many women bleached their hair to achieve a blonde color. This wear and tear on the hair due to dyeing and bleaching added to the continued popularity of the high forehead in fashion. The hairstyles at this time were often dictated by the large collars (ruffs and whisks) that were in fashion. This meant that many of the hairstyles had to be updos—you rarely see long flowing hair in this era. In order to keep things neat (as well as providing another place to decorate), the bun in the back of the hairstyle was often covered by a cloth cap or a jeweled net. Hairstyles were also designed to complement the fashionable hats of the time, especially the French hood (a half-moon-shaped hat) and the *atifet* (a heart-shaped crescent hat). The heart shape appears over and over again in the Elizabethan era. In both Figure 7.1 and 7.2 the silhouette of the hair has a defined heart shape. This was often accomplished by dressing the hair over hair pads, or, in more extreme cases, a wire frame.

    Another common shape during this era was a narrow, rounded oval shape (see Figure 7.3). Depending on how tall this shape was, it could have been dressed over either hair pads or a wire frame, too. The hairstyles (whether on natural hair or wigs) were styled with wax, starches, and gums. The excessive styling also led to frizzy hair textures.

Figure 7.3   Portrait of Amy Robsart, Lady Dudley (1532–60) (oil on canvas), English School (16th century) / Private Collection / The Bridgeman Art Library International. This portrait is an example of both the oval silhouette of the hairstyle and of the frizzy, tightly curled hair texture.

Elizabethan Men

The Elizabethan period had some of the greatest variety in historical men's hairstyles. At the beginning of this era, hair was often clipped quite short. As times passed in this period, the hair became longer. Late in the era, curls or waves in the hair were quite fashionable. Balding men at this time would sometimes wear wigs to keep up with the trend for full, flowing hair. In the 1590s, men began wearing lovelocks, a style in which one lock of hair (usually in front of the shoulder) was allowed to grow longer than the rest of the hair (see Figure 7.4). Lovelocks would become even more popular in the Cavalier era.

This time period for men also saw a great variety of facial hair. Beards and goatees of all shapes and sizes were found in this period. Most men had some sort of facial hair—clean-shaven looks were not particularly popular. A mustache and small goatee (like that in Figure 7.4) were very fashionable. Full beards that were longer on the chin and shorter on the jaw, such as that in Figure 7.5, can also been seen in many portraits from this era.

Figure 7.4 Portrait of Henry Wriothesley (1573–1624), 3rd Earl of Southampton c. 1600 (oil on canvas) (detail), English School, (17th century) / National Portrait Gallery, London, UK / The Bridgeman Art Library International. This portrait is an example of the fashionable, long wavy locks of hair worn by Elizabethan men. His facial hair is also quite typical of the time period.

Figure 7.5 Portrait of Thomas Pead, 1578 (oil on panel), Ketel, Cornelis (1548–1616) / © The Berger Collection at the Denver Art Museum, USA / The Bridgeman Art Library International. This portrait shows a shorter men's hairstyle and the fuller beard often seen in this period.

Elizabethan Woman's Styling—Step by Step Instructions

This hairstyle was inspired by the portrait of Queen Elizabeth I in Figure 7.1.

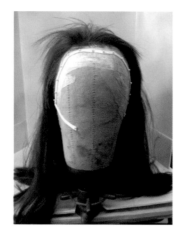

Figure 7.6   Step 1. Begin with a long wig that has some short pieces or bangs around the face. The length of the hair should be ideally four to eight inches around the face, and at least twelve inches in the back from the nape of the wig. I used a lace front wig made with synthetic hair. A shorter wig could be augmented with a switch in the back to form the bun as long as the rest of the hair in the wig is long enough to pull into a small ponytail at the back of the head. Both hard front wigs and lace front wigs work well for this hairstyle.

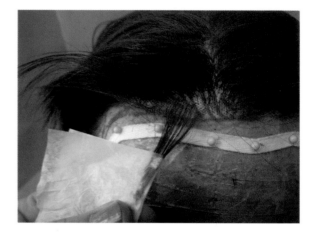

Figure 7.7   Step 2. Wet the front of the hair with setting lotion and section out a small piece to make a spit curl. Spit curls are small flat curls that lie against the face. (These curls would be very helpful in concealing the front edge of the wig if you are using a hard front wig.)

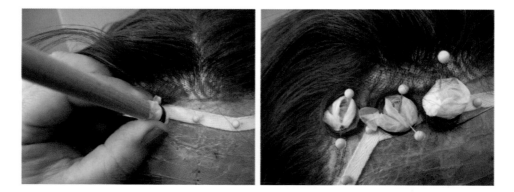

Figures 7.8 and 7.9   Step 3. Use a dowel rod to pin curl the hair along the hairline. Secure each curl with pins or clippies.

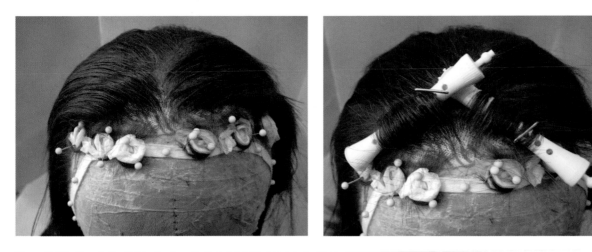

Figure 7.10   Step 4. The finished spit curls along the hairline.

Figure 7.11   Step 5. In order to get a lot of texture into the wig, I chose to set the front section on perm rods. Set the rods in a "V" shape to begin creating the heart shape of the hairstyle.

Figure 7.13   Step 7. Set a perm rod behind the "V" shape at the center front of the wig rolling back toward the crown of the head. This will help you avoid having an ugly gap when you are ready to style the wig.

Figure 7.12   Step 6. Continue setting rollers down the side of the front section, using pencil-sized rollers when you get a bit closer to the bottom.

Figure 7.14   Step 8. Set a few pencil rollers behind the first row of rollers, angling them toward the back of the wig.

Figure 7.15 Step 9. Pull the hair in the back of the wig smoothly into a ponytail. Notice how not all of the remaining hair is in this ponytail—some of the hair is still hanging down at the nape of the neck.

Figure 7.16 Step 10. Braid the hair in the ponytail into two rope braids.

Figures 7.17 and 7.18 Step 11. Secure the rope braids out of the way. Roll the hair at the nape of the wig up toward the ponytail.

Elizabethan Woman's Hairstyle—The Finished Set

Figures 7.19–24 The finished Elizabethan Woman's style set.

Once you have finished setting the wig, steam it if it is a synthetic wig or thoroughly wet it if it is a human hair wig. Put it in the wig dryer to dry for at least 75 minutes.

Figure 7.25   Step 12. Begin removing the rollers at the nape of the neck.

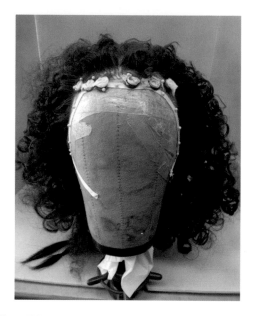

Figure 7.26   Step 13. The wig with all of the rollers removed. Leave the pin curls at the hairline set in place while styling the rest of the wig.

Figure 7.27   Step 14. Use a wide-toothed comb to gently comb through the tight curls around the front and nape of the wig.

Figure 7.28   Step 15. Use a teasing/smoothing brush to lightly tease the underside of each tightly curled section. This will help prevent roller breaks (unattractive gaps in the hairstyle that fall between where the rollers were).

Figure 7.29 Step 16. Sweep the left side of the back curly section up around to the right side of the ponytail containing the rope braids. Secure this section with bobby pins.

Figure 7.30 Step 17. Use a teasing comb to smooth out this section. Spray lightly with hairspray.

Figure 7.31 Step 18. Sweep the right side of the back curly section up around to the left side of the ponytail. Secure with bobby pins, smooth, and spray lightly with hairspray.

Figure 7.32 Step 19. Move back around to the front section of the wig. Take about one-third of the hair and pull it back toward the ponytail containing the rope braids. Secure with bobby pins.

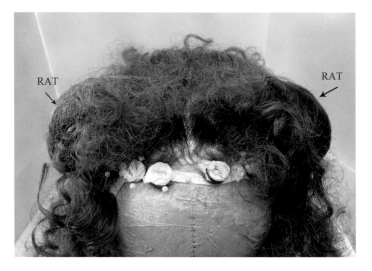

Figure 7.33   Step 20. Part the remaining hair in the front section in the center. Pin a hair rat behind either side of the front, creating a heart-shaped silhouette.

Figure 7.34   Step 21. Grasp the front section of hair at the sideburn on one side and twist it up and over the rat. Secure with bobby pins. Be sure not to pull this section so tight that all of the curly texture is pulled straight.

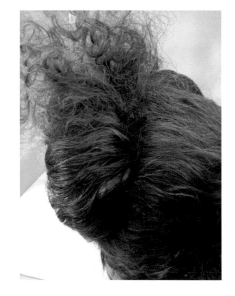

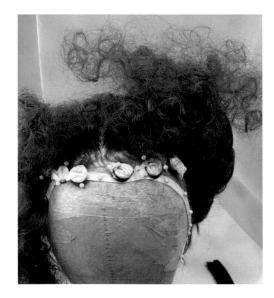

Figure 7.35   Step 22. The finished side, with the rat covered with the hair. Notice how the ends are left free and curly. Repeat on the other side of the wig.

Figure 7.36   Step 23. Front view of the pinned side with the ends of the hair left free.

Figure 7.37   Step 24. Front view after both sides have been pinned.

Figure 7.38   Step 25. You now need to arrange the remaining curls in the front section to look neat. Begin by combing individual curls around your finger with a rat tail comb.

Figure 7.39   Step 26. Place each curl gracefully and secure it into the hair rat with a hairpin.

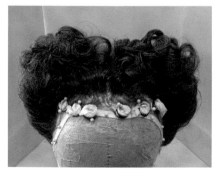

Figure 7.40   Step 27. The finished view of the neatly arranged front curls.

Figure 7.41   Step 28. There will now be a cloud of curls surrounding the ponytail with the rope braids.

Figure 7.42   Step 29. Neatly smooth and gather these curls until they form an attractive cluster. Make sure not to overwork these curls. Pin the cluster in place and further secure it with a hairnet.

Figure 7.43 Step 30. Wrap the rope braids around the curl cluster. Wrap one clockwise and the other counterclockwise.

Figure 7.44 Step 31. It is finally time to unpin the spit curls at the front. Remove the pins holding them in place and comb through them, being sure to maintain each individual curl.

Figure 7.45 Step 32. Use a small dab of white school glue on each curl. This will serve as your styling product. Washable school glue will not harm your wig and can be washed out later. You need to use the glue after setting because it will make your end paper stick to the hair or the roller.

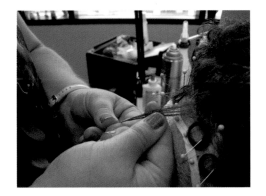

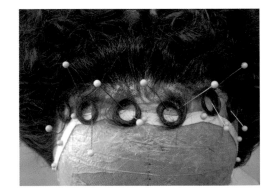

Figure 7.46 Step 33. Work the glue through each curl and pin it back in place.

Figure 7.47 Step 34. Leave the curls pinned in place and allow them to set in place overnight.

The wig style is now completed! You can accessorize the wig in any number of ways—the Elizabethan period was quite an extravagant one. Pearls, jewels, feathers, decorative nets, or a gold cording are all good options for Elizabethan décor.

Elizabethan Woman—The Completed Hairstyle

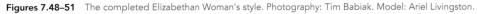

Figures 7.48–51   The completed Elizabethan Woman's style. Photography: Tim Babiak. Model: Ariel Livingston.

Variations

There are several ways to create variety in Elizabethan wig styles. The décor is an easy and obvious way. Although red was the most fashionable wig color, blonde hair still remained popular as well. You can vary the texture of your wigs—some could have very tight curls, and some could be very smooth. You could place your rats in the center of the wigs to create the more oval silhouette, seen in Figure 7.3, instead of using the popular heart-shaped silhouette.

Figures 7.52–53   Student Maur Sela models her version of an Elizabethan hairstyle.

Figure 7.54   Kim Adams models an Elizabethan style that has been styled with a hard front wig.

eight

THE CAVALIER/ JACOBEAN PERIOD

{ *1603–1660* }

Figure 8.1   Katherine (1609–67), Countess of Chesterfield, and Lucy (b. 1608), Countess of Huntingdon, c. 1636–40 (oil on canvas), Dyck, Sir Anthony van (1599–1641) / Yale Center for British Art, Paul Mellon Collection, USA / The Bridgeman Art Library.

Important Events

1603	James I becomes King of England
1605	Guy Fawkes tries to blow up the English Parliament in the Gunpowder Plot
1607	English colony at Jamestown Virginia is established
1611	King James Bible is published
1616	William Shakespeare dies
1620	Pilgrims land at Plymouth Rock
1632	Work begins on the Taj Mahal
1649	King Charles I is executed
1649–1660	Time of the Commonwealth in England

Important Artists/Designers

William Dobson, Franz Hals, Inigo Jones, Anthony Van Dyck, Rembrandt van Rijn, Peter Paul Rubens, Diego Rodrigo de Silva y Velazquez.

Important People/Style Icons

King Charles I, Oliver Cromwell, Queen Henrietta Maria, King James, Elisabeth of France—Queen of Spain, Elizabeth and Frederick—King and Queen of Bohemia, French Musketeers

Cavalier/Jacobean Women

In the Cavalier era, women's hairstyles became softer and simpler. The stiff, heart-shaped red wigs of the Elizabethan era gave way to looser ringlets and natural hair colors. The large dramatic hats that were popular in this period would not fit over a stiff, structured hairstyle, so the hairstyles become much flatter on top in order to accommodate the hats. Women's hair in this period was usually pulled straight off the forehead in the center and long curls were left to hang over the ears on each side (see Figure 8.2).

Figure 8.2 Jane Needham, Mrs Middleton, c. 1663–65 (oil on canvas), Lely, Sir Peter (1618–80) / The Royal Collection © 2011 Her Majesty Queen Elizabeth II / The Bridgeman Art Library. This portrait shows the long curls and pulled-back center section typical of Cavalier period hairstyles. Also notice the shorter curls on the forehead.

There was often a fringe of short bangs or spit curls on the forehead. In many ways, this hairstyle made a woman resemble a King Charles spaniel, a dog that was wildly popular at this time. The long curly ears of the dog were very similar to the curls hanging over each ear on a woman's hairstyle.

On the back of the head, women's hairstyles were usually pulled into a simple bun just below the crown (see Figure 8.3). The bun was often coiled hair arranged in concentric circles, and might be decorated with pearls, cords, or a simple net covering.

The hair in the back might also have a loose section of long curls at the nape of the neck. The curls might be evenly full, such as in Figure 8.2, or they might be more asymmetrical, falling over one shoulder as in Figure 8.4.

Figure 8.4   Portait of Queen Consort Henrietta Maria of France, Anthony van Dyck, 1632–35. This portrait shows Henrietta Maria with a lovelock of curls falling over one shoulder.

Figure 8.3   *Man and Woman Sitting at the Virginal*, Gabriel Metsu, 1658–60. This painting illustrates the typical bun placement on women's hairstyles in this period.

Cavalier/Jacobean Men

Men's hairstyles during this era were growing longer, and were quite dashing. These hairstyles were often longer on one side. The longer hair was sometimes arranged into a "lovelock," a carefully styled curl that lay on one shoulder (see Figure 8.5). These hairstyles might also have a short fringe of bangs, or be swept off of the forehead, sometimes with a center part.

This long hair usually hung down over a large falling collar trimmed with lace. Facial hair was very popular during this period. Carefully groomed mustaches that flipped up dramatically at the ends were worn with either tufts of hair directly under the lower lip (sometimes called a "French dot"), or a small, sharply pointed goatee (see Figure 8.6). These goatees are often called "Van Dyck beards," so called after artist Anthony van Dyck , who featured them in many of his portraits.

Figure 8.5 Sir Francis Godolphin, 1633 (oil on canvas), Janssen van Ceulen, Cornelius (1593–1661) / Yale Center for British Art, Paul Mellon Collection, USA / The Bridgeman Art Library. This portrait shows a fringed Cavalier hairstyle with a lovelock on one side.

Figure 8.6 *Charles I, King of England, from Three Angles*, the Triple Portrait by Anthony van Dyck. This portrait shows Charles I wearing typical facial hair and the sweeping asymmetrical hairstyle of the Cavalier period

Cavalier Woman's Styling—Step by Step Instructions

The visual inspiration for this hairstyle was taken from the woman on the left in Figure 8.1 (wearing the silver-gray dress).

Figure 8.7   Step 1. Begin with a wig that is long in the back (12 inches at the nape of the neck) with layers (six to eight inches) around the face. Small wisps of hair or a fringe on the forehead is ideal for this style. I used a lace front wig made of synthetic hair.

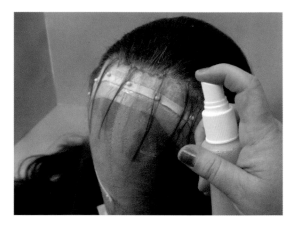

Figure 8.8   Step 2. Wet the wisps of hair on the forehead with setting lotion. If the wig you are using has short bangs all the way across, you will want to sweep some of the hair back into the rest of the style so that the forehead does not become overwhelmed with curls.

Figure 8.9   Step 3. Use a wooden dowel rod or your fingers to shape the wisps of hair into spit curls.

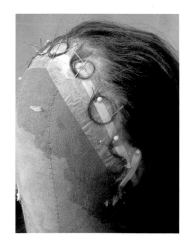

Figure 8.10   Step 4. Notice how some of the curls are set going toward the face, some curl away from the face, and some of the curls have more of an "S" shape.

Figure 8.11 Step 5. Pull the top center section of hair straight back off the forehead. Anchor this hair in a ponytail that sits just below the crown of the head.

Figure 8.12 Step 6. Begin setting the side section of hair on dime-sized rollers that are rolling away from the face.

Figure 8.13 Step 7. If there are any short wisps of hair behind the ears, set them on medium-sized perm rods.

Figure 8.14 Step 8. Set another row of side curls on dime-sized rollers, this time setting the rollers going toward the face.

Figure 8.15 Step 9. Make a second ponytail in the center back of the head just below the first ponytail you made. Leave some hair out of the ponytail on one side—this hair will form the longer curls that will hang over one shoulder. Pin the hair in both ponytails up and out of the way with a duckbill clip. Set a section of hair behind the ear on each side of the head on a nickel-sized roller—set this section rolling up toward the center of the head. Set the hair you kept out of the ponytail for longer curls or a lovelock on dime-sized rollers.

Cavalier Woman's Hairstyle—The Finished Set

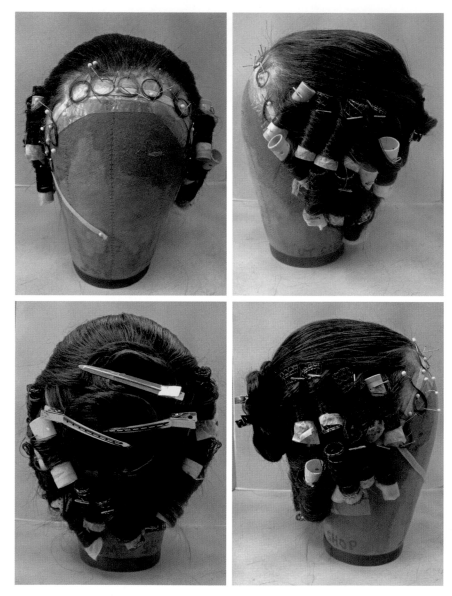

Figures 8.16–19   The finished Cavalier Woman's style set.

Once you have finished setting the wig, steam each roller thoroughly if the wig is made of synthetic hair. If the wig is human hair, soak each roller with water from a spray bottle. After steaming or wetting, place the wig in a wig dryer for 75 minutes.

To style:

Figure 8.20   Step 10. Remove all of the rollers from the wig, beginning at the nape of the neck.

Figure 8.21   Step 11. Use a teasing/smoothing brush to lightly tease the loose section of hair behind each ear.

Figure 8.22   Step 12. Pull each of these sections of hair diagonally up across the back of the head and pin them next to the ponytails on the opposite side of the head.

Figure 8.23   Step 13. Take the ponytails down from the duckbill clips.

Figure 8.24   Step 14. Take the loose ends of the sections you just pinned up, twist them, and pin the twisted hair around the two ponytails.

Figure 8.25   Step 15. Twist the top ponytail and wind it into a round bun, pinning the hair with bobby pins as you go.

Figure 8.26   Step 16. Twist the bottom ponytail and wrap that hair around the outside of the bun, again pinning the hair with bobby pins. Tuck the end of the twisted ponytail under the bun so that it is hidden.

Figure 8.27   Step 17. Use a hairnet to make the bun look neat and to hold it together. You could also decorate the bun at this time if you desire.

Figure 8.28   Step 18. Move to the side curls of hair. Brush through each curl, lightly tease the hair, and mist it with hairspray.

Figure 8.29 Step 19. After you mist the section with hairspray, brush the hair around a dowel rod to form it into a ringlet. Gently slide the dowel rod out once the curl is formed.

Figure 8.30 Step 20. If a ringlet is longer than you want it to be, loop the top couple of inches around your finger, drawing up the hair.

Figure 8.31 Step 21. Pin the loop/knot of hair you have formed with a bobby pin, taking care to make the knot pretty. This trick is very useful if you are using a long wig that you do not want to cut shorter around the face.

Figure 8.32 Step 22. To dress the curls at the nape of the neck, brush each section around your finger and mist with hairspray. Let them hang down loose so that they blend in with the ringlets on the left side of the wig.

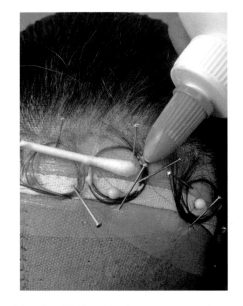

Figure 8.33 Step 23. Use white glue on a cotton swab to make the spit curls at the front of the wig hold their shape. White school glue is an excellent styling tool to use on small curls, and washes out of the wig with shampoo.

Cavalier Woman—The Completed Hairstyle

Figures 8.34–37   The completed Cavalier Woman's style. Photography: Tim Babiak. Model: Josephine McAdam.

Variations

You can vary your Cavalier women's looks by using a fringe of bangs instead of sculpted spit curls on the forehead. You can also create a much fuller hairstyle by putting less hair in the bun and letting more hair hang down in the back or around the face.

Figure 8.38 Lexi O'Reilly styled and models a version of the Cavalier hairstyle that is fuller with more ringlets hanging down.

You can also create a simper version of this hairstyle by using less hair over the ears, such as in the style seen in Figure 8.3.

Cavalier Man's Styling— Step by Step Instructions

This style is modeled after the portrait in Figure 8.5.

Figure 8.39 Step 1. Begin with a wig that is shoulder length with bangs. This wig is a hard front synthetic wig.

Figure 8.40 Step 2. Divide out the top section of the bangs and pin the hair out of the way for the moment. Set the lower section of bangs on nickel-sized rollers.

Figure 8.41   Step 3. Now set the top section of bangs on a nickel-sized roller.

Figure 8.42   Step 4. Use nickel-sized rollers to set spiral curls in diagonal rows. Use fairly large sections of hair so that the end result will be more of a wave than a curl. Notice how there is drag at the top of the rollers so that the top of the head is mostly flat. On the left side of the wig, also set the longer hair rolling toward the face on nickel-sized rollers. (These are the three rollers set vertically in this picture.) This hair will eventually become the "lovelock."

Figure 8.43   Step 5. Set the top section of hair on the right side of the head in the same large spiral curls rolling toward the face that you made on the left side of the wig. On the lower section of the wig on this side, set the hair around the face on dime-sized rollers. The tighter curl will help the hair appear shorter on that side, creating the asymmetry typical of Cavalier men's styles.

Figure 8.44   Step 6. On the center back of the wig, set a horizontal nickel-sized roller that will make the transition between the two sides. Continue setting the back of the wig with nickel-sized spiral curls, alternating the direction of diagonal rows down toward the nape.

Figure 8.45   Step 7. At the nape of the neck, switch to using dime-sized rollers, but still set the hair using the spiral curl technique.

Cavalier Man's Hairstyle—The Finished Set

Figures 8.46–49 The finished Cavalier Man's style set.

Once you have finished setting the wig, steam each roller thoroughly if the wig is made of synthetic hair. If the wig is human hair, soak each roller with water from a spray bottle. After steaming or wetting, place the wig in a wig dryer for 75 minutes.

To style:

Figure 8.50   Step 8. Remove all of the rollers from the wig, beginning at the nape of the neck. Brush through the entire wig with a large hairbrush.

Figure 8.51   Step 9. Form the lovelock on the longer left side of the wig by brushing the ends of the hair around your finger with a teasing/smoothing brush.

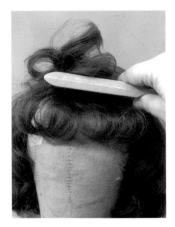

Figure 8.52   Step 10. To break up the roller marks in the bangs, lightly tease the hair and mist with hairspray. Smooth the bangs back down over the forehead with a smoothing brush.

Figure 8.53   Step 11. Men's wigs often look too fluffy or curly when they are taken out of rollers. To decrease the volume in the wig, use a brush or comb to pull the top part of the hair taut. Pass a steamer over the area so that the steam just briefly touches the hair. Do not let the steamer rest in front of any section of hair. Rather, keep the steamer moving so that it quickly passes over the hair. The steamer will help straighten the hair a little so that it does not have so much volume. You also do not want to lose the curls at the ends of the hair, so keep the steamer focused on the top half of the hair. Once you have lightly steamed the wig, brush through it again with a large brush.

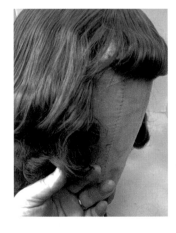

Figure 8.54   Step 12. To make one side look shorter than the other, brush the front section of hair around two fingers with a teasing/smoothing brush and pin the curl in place with a bobby pin. Make sure that the bobby pin is hidden from view.

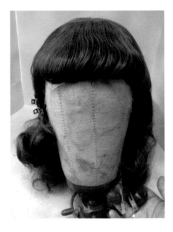

Figure 8.55   Step 13. Use clippies to help shape your wig into the desired final look. On the left side of this wig, curl clips are being used to hold the wig flatter to the head, which helps make a wig look more masculine and realistic. On the right side of this wig, curl clips are being used to add weight to the longer curls and pull them a bit longer in length. Whenever you are using curl clips this way, mist the sections of hair with hairspray and allow them to set.

Cavalier Man—The Completed Hairstyle

Figures 8.56–59   The completed Cavalier Man's style. Photography: Tim Babiak. Model: Leslie Hethcox.

Variations

Experimenting with texture will allow you to create a lot of character in your Cavalier men's looks. You can use straighter, shaggier textured hair (such as in Figure 8.3) to make a more rustic version of this look. Curlier versions of this look (such as in Figure 8.60) can make your character look more youthful or foppish. Using facial hair to accentuate this hairstyle can also make a statement about the character you are creating.

Figure 8.60   This painting shows two Cavalier men wearing a curlier version of a hairstyle from this period.

nine

THE RESTORATION/ BAROQUE ERA

{ *1660–1710* }

Figure 9.1   Portrait of a lady, half length, in a white and gold embroidered dress, with flowers in her hair (oil on canvas), Largillière, Nicolas de (1656–1746) / Private Collection / Photo © Christie's Images / The Bridgeman Art Library.

Important Events

1660   Charles II is restored to the throne of England

1660   Margaret Hughes becomes the first woman to act onstage, playing Desdemona in *Othello*

1666   The Great Fire of London

1670   Secret treaty of Dover between Charles II and Louis XIV bringing Roman Catholicism back to England

1676   Bacon's Rebellion breaks out in Virginia

1689   William and Mary become joint monarchs of England

1692   The Salem Witch trials are carried out in Massachusetts

1700   William Congreve's *The Way of the World* is first produced

Important Artists/Designers

Gian Lorenzo Bernini, Nicolas de Largilliere, Charles le Brun, Sir Peter Lely, Hyacinthe Rigaud, Jan Vermeer.

Important People/Style Icons

Aphra Behn, Charles II, William Congreve, Duchesse de Fontanges, Nell Gwynne, Louis XIV, Mary II of England, Isaac Newton, Barbara Villiers.

Restoration/Baroque Women

From 1649 to 1660, England was under the control of Oliver Cromwell and the "Roundheads," making up a government called the Protectorate or the Commonwealth. The Roundheads were so called because of their short, rounded haircuts. They were very sober people, with many rules regarding fashion and behavior. Once Charles II was restored to the throne in 1660, excess returned to fashion in full force. Women favored an excessive, romantic look. The shorter curls from the previous period grew longer and were allowed to hang down in the back and sometimes drape saucily over a shoulder. One popular hairstyle was called the *hurluberlu*, a style characterized by loops of curls around the head with longer ringlets hanging down the back (see Figure 9.2).

Figure 9.2 Portrait of Suzanna Doublet-Huygens (1637–1725), fifth and last child of Constantijn Huygens and Suzanna van Baerle, and their only daughter, painted by Caspar Netscher. This portrait shows an example of the hurluberlu hairstyle.

As this time period progressed, women's hairstyles got much sleeker on the sides, with the volume moving up to the top of the head (see Figure 9.3). To create this volume, women sometimes used false curls on top of their heads. They also sometimes used egg whites to add stiffness to the hair. Late in this period, women began powdering their hair, but both powdered looks and natural colors were equally in vogue.

Another popular hairstyle for women was the *Fontange*. This style was named for the Duchesse de Fontanges who had her hat blown off at a hunting party. She tied her curls up on top of her head with her ribbon garter. This kicked off a fashion for a hairstyle consisting of stiff wired curls that were stacked on top of each other. Later, this term also was used for a tall headpiece made of stiff wired fabric. The headpiece could now be used to add volume and height instead of having to achieve this effect with curls. This hairstyle was also characterized by two small curls at the temples, referred to as *favorites* (see Figure 9.4).

Figure 9.3 Mother and daughter, after Nicolas de Largillière (1656–1746) (colour litho), Devambez (19th century) / Bibliothèque des Arts Decoratifs, Paris, France / The Bridgeman Art Library. This mother and daughter both wear the stiffer, tall hair that was fashionable in this period.

Figure 9.4 Marie Marguerite Arouet (nee d'Aumart), c. 1700 (oil on canvas), Largillière, Nicolas de (1656–1746) / Private Collection / The Bridgeman Art Library. This portrait, as well as Figures 9.1 and 9.3, is an example of the fontange hairstyle.

Restoration/Baroque Men

Wigs were very common for men during this period, and they were usually worn over a shaved head. These wigs were sometimes called periwigs, or full bottom wigs. These wigs usually consisted of a long section of hair that hung over each shoulder in front, and one long section that hung down in the back (see Figure 9.5). Both Charles II and Louis XIV wore wigs to cover baldness; this greatly increased the popularity of wigs throughout the courts.

These wigs usually had a center part with two mounds of curls on top. By the 1690s, the center part became more defined, with the mounds of curls on either side taking on a pointed shape, as seen in Figure 9.6.

Figure 9.6 Sir Richard Carew, English School (17th century) / Antony House, Cornwall, UK / National Trust Photographic Library / John Hammond / The Bridgeman Art Library. This portrait shows a man with a very wide center part and more pointed mounds of hair on top.

Men's wigs became so tall that it was difficult for men to wear hats, and they carried them under their arms instead. Men also became somewhat casual about their wigs, and sometimes walked around with their wigs askew (see Figure 9.7).

Figure 9.5 *Portrait of a Nobleman*, Mignard, Pierre (1612–95) / Private Collection / Photo © Bonhams, London, UK / The Bridgeman Art Library. This portrait show an example of a full bottom wig. Also notice the faintest hint of a mustache on this man.

Figure 9.7   Portrait of John Dandridge (oil on canvas), English School (20th century) / Virginia Historical Society, Richmond, Virginia, USA / The Bridgeman Art Library. This portrait shows the subject's wig sliding back off his head, with the front of his own hairline visible.

Dark wig colors were the most popular, with hair powder gaining in popularity late in this period. Men were usually clean-shaven during this period. If any facial hair existed, it was usually in the form of an extremely tiny, thin mustache, such as that seen in Figure 9.5. Both men and women wore makeup during this period, with pale skin and rosy cheeks being preferred. Both genders also adopted the fashion of wearing small cloth patches on their faces; these patches were originally worn to cover smallpox scars.

Restoration Woman's Fontange Styling— Step by Step Instructions

I used Figure 9.1 as my reference for this hairstyle.

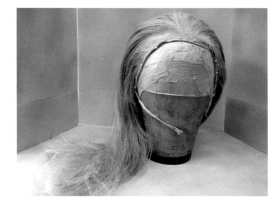

Figure 9.8   Step 1. Begin with a long, mostly one-length wig (at least 14 inches long at the nape of the neck is ideal) that has short pieces around the face. The forehead curls can be trimmed into the wig if they are not already present. I used a long, gray, synthetic, lace front wig.

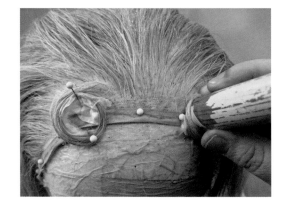

Figure 9.9   Step 2. Use a wooden dowel rod to form pin curls on the temples. (These are the curls known as *favorites*.)

Figure 9.10 Step 3. Use a dime-sized roller to roll the center section of hair on the base straight back. Next, set a dime-sized roller at an angle on each side of the center roller. Set a perm rod with a small section of hair rolling forward just in front of each ear. Finally, use a quarter-sized roller to roll the sides back. Put a little bit of drag on these rollers to keep the hairstyle nice and tight on the sides.

Figure 9.11 Step 4. Continue setting the top section of the wig on dime-sized rollers, set in a brick pattern.

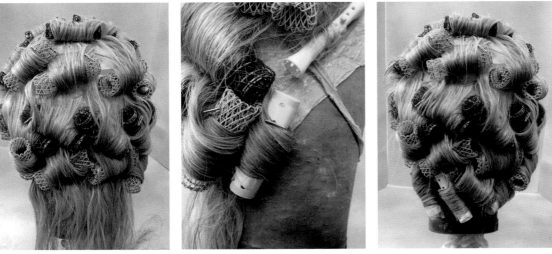

Figure 9.12 Step 5. Once you reach the crown of the head, switch to using quarter-sized rollers. Set these rollers in diagonal rows, with each row alternating direction.

Figure 9.13 Step 6. Behind each ear, set a curl on a dime-sized roller rolling toward the face.

Figure 9.14 Step 7. Set the bottom row of curls on dime-sized rollers. These curls will become the ringlets hanging down the back.

Restoration Woman's Fontange Hairstyle—The Finished Set

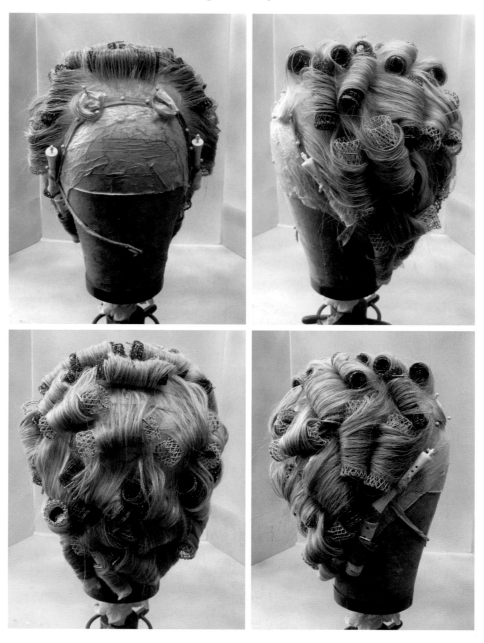

Figures 9.15–18   The finished Restoration Woman's Fontange style set.

Once you have finished setting the wig, steam each roller thoroughly if the wig is made of synthetic hair. If the wig is human hair, soak each roller with water from a spray bottle. After steaming or wetting, place the wig in a wig dryer for 75 minutes.

To style:

Figure 9.19   Step 8. Remove all of the rollers from the wig beginning at the nape of the neck. For now, leave the curls on the forehead pinned in place.

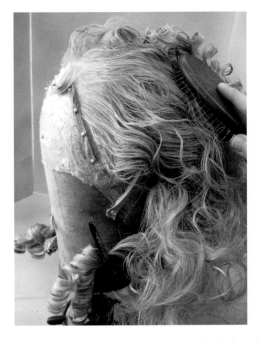

Figure 9.20   Step 9. Use a large wooden brush to brush through all of the wig, except for the bottom row of dime-sized curls. Pull these curls forward and secure them out of the way with duckbill clips so they will not get mixed in with the rest of the hair.

Figure 9.21   Step 10. Use a teasing brush to tease the front center section of hair. Be sure to spray between each section as you tease. This will help the entire hairstyle stick together.

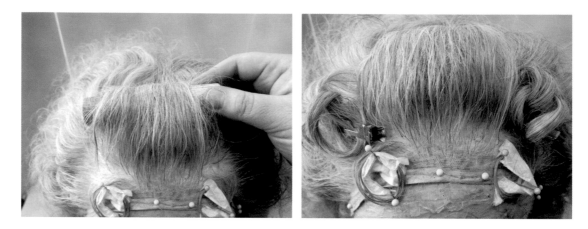

Figures 9.22 and 9.23   Step 11. Use a dowel rod to roll the front section of hair back. Pin the rolled hair in place with silver bobby pins.

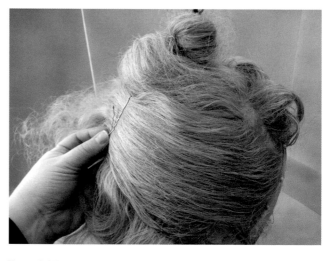

Figure 9.24   Step 12. Pull all of the curls around the center section up and pin them out of the way for now.

Figure 9.25   Step 13. Smooth the side sections of hair back and pin them at the center of the head.

Figure 9.26   Step 14. Pin the ends of each side section up toward the crown of the head.

Figure 9.27   Step 15. Sweep the rest of the hair over to one side, and secure the hair up the center back with crossed bobby pins.

Figure 9.28   Step 16. Roll the hair in the back of the head into a French twist. A French twist is made by gathering the hair in your hand, twisting it, and then twisting the coil up toward the crown of the head. Secure the twist with bobby pins.

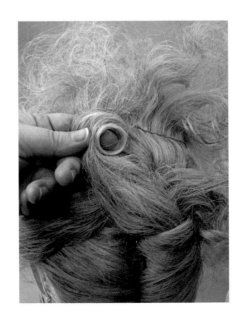

Figure 9.29   Step 17. Form the tail of the French twist into a curl and pin it in place with a bobby pin.

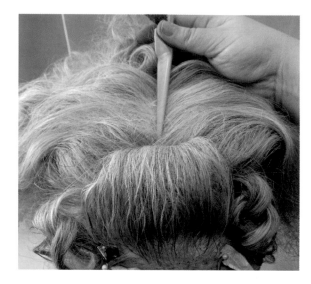

Figure 9.30 Step 18. Return to the front section of the hair. Make a center part in the top section.

Figure 9.31 Step 19. Form the hair on either side of the part into rolls, using the dowel rod.

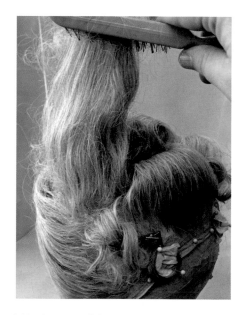

Figure 9.32 Step 20. Pull the next section up and lightly tease it on the inside so that the teased side will be hidden when you roll the hair around the dowel rod.

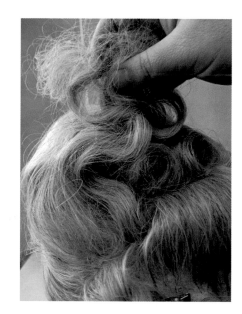

Figure 9.33 Step 21. Drape the section of hair over the center curls, allowing the wave shape to remain in the hair. Pin the middle of this section to the center roll.

Figure 9.34 Step 22. You will now have two loose fuzzy sections of hair on top of the first two rolled curls. Form these curls into a second set of rolls.

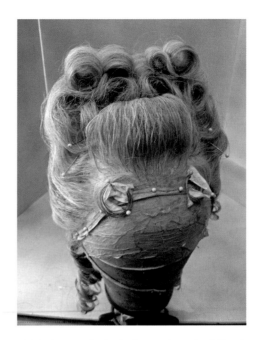

Figure 9.35 Step 23. The finished set of shaped, rolled curls.

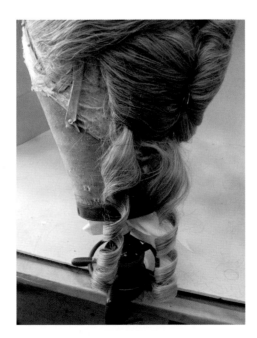

Figure 9.36 Step 24. Shape the curls at the nape of the neck into ringlets by brushing the curls around your finger or around a dowel rod.

Restoration Woman's Fontange—The Completed Hairstyle

Figures 9.37–40   The completed Restoration Woman's Fontange style. Photography: Tim Babiak. Model: Sabrina Lotfi.

Variations

Natural hair colors were as fashionable in this period as powdered hair, so you can use both to create variety in your Restoration wigs. Adding a fabric fontange headpiece is another way to add the illusion of height to these wigs. You can also style a wig in the *hurluberlu* style as another option for the Baroque period.

Figures 9.41 and 9.42   Bethany Renfro models her hurluberlu-styled wig. She has incorporated ribbon loop accents in her final look.

Man's Full Bottom Wig Styling—
Step by Step Instructions

This wig look is based on the wig the gentleman is wearing in Figure 9.5. Before you beginning setting a full bottom wig, you must have the proper wig to start with. I like to create full bottom wigs by purchasing two wigs in the same color and cutting up one to use as parts. The ideal wig to purchase will be very full, with long layers (at least eight inches long) all over the head. The wig will need pieces that hang over in front of each shoulder.

Figure 9.43   Step 1. Begin by creating a pattern piece for the section of hair sitting in front of the shoulder. First, I laid out a piece of plastic wrap and covered it with clear tape to add stability. I held this piece of plastic up to my performer and roughly marked out how large I wanted this piece to be in order to form a panel that would hang over his shoulder. I then cleaned this pattern up and made a neater version. Cut out two of these shapes in cotton netting or muslin that has been dyed to be the same color as the hair in the wig. I used caul net, a wig-making net with large diamond-shaped holes.

Figure 9.44   Step 2. Stitch rows of weft taken from the second wig onto each pattern piece. You remove the weft from the second wig by using a seam ripper to remove each individual row. Another option is to use scissors to cut the second wig into large chunks and sew those chunks directly to your pattern piece.

Figure 9.45   Step 3. Stitch the pattern piece with weft into the base of the first wig. It should be attached into the wig just in front of the ears on either side. Fill in any gaps with extra weft. Here, you can see the partial lace front that I also added to this wig.

Figure 9.46   Step 4. An inside view of the wig with the extra pieces attached.

Figure 9.47 Step 5. I blocked this wig on a long-necked canvas wig block so that I would have extra room to pin rollers. This wig is a full bottom synthetic wig with a partial lace front. Make a center part in the wig with a rat tail comb.

Figure 9.48 Step 6. Use pencil-sized perm rods to begin setting curls on either side of the part.

Figure 9.49 Step 7. Continue setting small rollers all the way down to the bottom of the added piece.

Figure 9.50 Step 8. Set more perm rods at the crown of the head. Continue setting the hair in the rest of the wig on pencil- and dime-sized rollers.

Man's Full Bottom Wig—The Finished Set

Figures 9.51–54   The finished Man's Full Bottom Wig style set.

Once you have finished setting the wig, steam each roller thoroughly if the wig is made of synthetic hair. If the wig is human hair, soak each roller with water from a spray bottle. After steaming or wetting, place the wig in a wig dryer for 75 minutes.

To style:

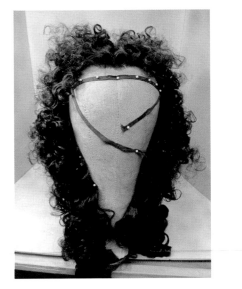

Figure 9.55   Step 9. Remove all of the rollers from the wig, beginning at the bottom/nape and working your way up toward the crown.

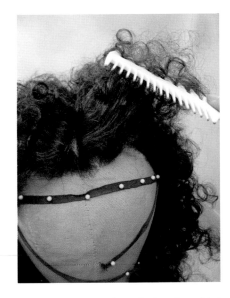

Figure 9.56   Step 10. Use a wide-toothed comb to pick through all of the hair in the wig.

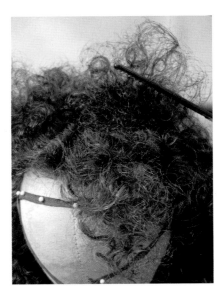

Figure 9.57   Step 11. Use a teasing comb to backcomb the hair in the front of the wig. Spray the hair with hairspray as you tease the section in order to make the hair stick together.

Figure 9.58   Step 12. Smooth the front section of hair upwards from the face, forming a peak. Shape the entire section of hair into a mound.

Figure 9.59   Step 13. Work your way down the side sections of hair, teasing the hair so that there are no roller breaks.

Figure 9.60   Step 14. Shape the curls at the bottom of the wig (both at the nape of the neck and at the front sections) by brushing the curls around your finger.

Figure 9.61   Step 15. Emphasize the center part by pinning tapes down the center of the front section. Mist the wig with hairspray and let it set overnight.

Man's Full Bottom Wig—The Completed Hairstyle

Figures 9.62–65   The completed Man's Full Bottom Wig style. Photography: Tim Babiak. Model: Leslie Hethcox.

Variations

Like the women's wigs from this period, men's wigs can be either natural hair colors, or a powdered gray color. You can also shape the curls in a much more rigid manner to create variety. A particularly foppish character might decorate the front sections of his wig with bows.

ten

THE GEORGIAN/ ROCOCO PERIOD

{ *1710–1789* }

Figure 10.1   Portrait of Marie Antoinette de Habsbourg-Lorraine (1755–93) (oil on canvas), French School (18th century) / Musee Antoine Lecuyer, Saint-Quentin, France / The Bridgeman Art Library International.

Georgian/Rococo Women

Rococo art and architecture was ornate, full of curves, heavily gilded with gold, used a great deal of pastel colors, and was often asymmetrical. In many ways, this was also true of fashions in hair and clothing. The hair in this period reached new heights (literally) in elaborate hairstyling and ornamentation. Much of the hair was structured like architecture, with rolls and curls dressed over frames and pads to help these styles reach the sky.

Hair at the beginning of this period started out with a simpler silhouette (see Figure 10.2).

Figure 10.2   Harriot Walter (1756–86), 3rd Viscountess Grimston (oil on canvas) / Private Collection / The Bridgeman Art Library International. This woman's hairstyle is worn relatively close to her head. It is ornamented with small jewels and a feather.

Madame du Pompadour helped to make this simpler silhouette popular. The hairstyles had a slight pouf of fullness at the center front, which gave the pompadour its name. (The pompadour hairstyles in this period are not nearly as extreme as what the pompadour would become in the 1950s.)

In the 1770s and 1780s, the French court became the epicenter of fashion. Marie Antoinette and her elaborately dressed coiffures set the fashion that other members of the court scrambled to keep up with. An example of Marie Antoinette's tall, bejeweled, and plumed hairstyle can be seen in Figure 10.1. This type of hairstyle was achieved by dressing the hair over wire frames and hair pads. Artificial hair was also incorporated into these styles to add volume and height. Hair powder for both men and women became fashionable at this time. The powder was usually made of finely ground starch. It was most often used in its natural off-white color (see Figure 10.3), but was also sometimes tinted in pastel colors to complement the fashions of the day.

The decorations at this time became so outlandish that courtiers competed with each other over who could have the most elaborately themed hairstyle. One famous example is that of the "*Coiffure à l'Indépendance ou le Triomphe de la liberté*" (Figure 10.4). Wigs decorated like this is where the term "ship wig" comes from.

Figure 10.3   *The Ladies Waldegrave*, 1780 (oil on canvas), Reynolds, Sir Joshua (1723–92) / © National Gallery of Scotland, Edinburgh, Scotland / The Bridgeman Art Library International. These ladies sport both powdered hair and tall hairstyles, likely dressed over a wire frame. Note the varieties in rolls, clubs, and curls in the backs of the styles.

Figure 10.4   The "Coiffure à l'Indépendance ou le Triomphe de la liberté" was an elaborate French hairstyle designed to commemorate a victory in the American Revolution.

Wigs were so expensive and such a status symbol at the time that there were actually wig thieves who stole wigs and sold them. They would snatch wigs from perches on top of a wall as people walked by; other thieves would steal wigs by cutting holes in the back of carriages and stealing the wigs from behind.

Later in this period, as civil unrest and rage at the wealthy was growing, hairstyles became simpler again. Elaborate hairstyles were let go in favor of elaborate hats and turbans (see Figure 10.5). This "country" look was also made popular by Marie Antoinette, who sometimes enjoyed dressing as a shepherdess. Straw bonnets and elaborate mob caps were common.

Figure 10.5 The Marquise de Pezay (or Pezé), and the Marquise de Rougé with Her Sons Alexis and Adrien, 1787, (oil on canvas), painted by Elisabeth Vigée Le Brun / National Gallery of Art. This portrait shows an example of both an elaborate mob cap and a turban.

Another important hairstyle in this period was the hedgehog hairstyle. The hedgehog consisted of an elaborate cloud of curls around the face with long ringlets hanging down in the back. An example can be seen in Figure 10.6. A large hat was often perched at an angle on this hairstyle.

Figure 10.6 Portrait of Georgiana, Duchess of Devonshire, c. 1785–87 (oil on canvas), Gainsborough, Thomas (1727–88) / Chatsworth House, Derbyshire, UK / © Devonshire Collection, Chatsworth / Reproduced by permission of Chatsworth Settlement Trustees / The Bridgeman Art Library International.

Georgian/Rococo Men

Men's hairstyles in this period started out simpler than they ended it. Men were usually still wearing wigs, but they were much smaller and more contained than in the Baroque period. The hair was usually dressed back in a queue (a ponytail at the nape of the neck), with a slight pompadour in the front of the wig, and rolls at the sides of the wig by the ears. Figure 10.7 is an example of a typical hair fashion for this period.

Just as women began powdering their hair in the middle of this period, so did the men. Getting dressed and styling the hair was an elaborate ritual. A man's valet would often do the actual powdering while the gentleman held a cone in front of his face to keep his face clean and to avoid inhaling the powder. This can be seen in Figure 10.8.

Figure 10.8 *The Toilet of an Attorney's Clerk*, engraved by Philibert Louis Debucourt (1755–1832) (engraving), Vernet, Antoine Charles Horace (Carle) (1758–1836) (after) / Private Collection / The Stapleton Collection / The Bridgeman Art Library International.

Figure 10.7 Reginald Pole Carew, 1773 (oil on canvas), Wyrsch or Wursch, Johann Melchior Joseph (1732–98) / Antony House, Cornwall, UK / National Trust Photographic Library / John Hammond / The Bridgeman Art Library International.

This hairstyle was often accented by a simple grosgrain ribbon around the queue.

As you can imagine, this powder often got messy. Men began wearing a black velvet bag to cover the ponytail and to prevent the powder from getting on the back of their expensive coats. These bags became a fashion statement in and of themselves.

Figure 10.9 Portrait of George III of the United Kingdom, 1762, by Allan Ramsey. King George is wearing a wig bag on his queue.

Figure 10.10 Pantheon Macaroni, 1773 (oil on canvas) (b/w photo), English School (18th century) / Private Collection / The Bridgeman Art Library International. A caricature of a typical macaroni.

Also like the women's wigs of this period, men's wigs grew more and more elaborate. They were dressed very high, often with a pointed cone shape to the front section. The fashion for side rolls continued (see Figure 10.9), but rolls in the back were also now part of the style. The queues became elaborate and the wig bags more decorative. The hair was sometimes dressed in a club in the back—a club was a ponytail that was folded back on itself and tied in the center, forming a loop above and below the tie. Hats were also a part of this fashion, ranging from tiny hats that perched on top of the tall wigs, to simple tricorns that men sometimes just carried under their arm so as not to mess up their wig. Men who took these fashions to extremes were referred to as macaronis, a term taken from the Italian word *maccherone*, which means "blockhead" or "fool" (see Figure 10.10).

Men's wig styles at this time were often dictated by profession. Military men often wore their queues tightly wrapped in grosgrain ribbon, forming a sort of rat tail. There were specific wigs for other professions, such as clergy, marriage brokers, barristers, and judges. The last gasp of these wig styles can be seen today in the wigs still worn by barristers and judges in British courts.

Once a gentleman or lady of the house was finished wearing his or her wig, it was then passed down to the servants. The more important the servant, the better quality of wig they had. The wealthy often had wigs made of human hair or fine yak hair. Poorer people had to make do with lesser materials for their wigs, such as horse hair or badger hair. Some people even resorted to cotton in an attempt to replicate fashionable wig styles.

Figure 10.11 *Heads of Six of Hogarth's Servants*, mid-1750s, by William Hogarth. These servants wear simpler hairstyles than the wealthy people in this period wore. The men are still emulating the looks of the wigs in this period.

Woman's Georgian/Rococo Styling—Step by Step Instructions

This hairstyle is modeled after Figure 10.1. Before you can begin styling your Marie Antoinette-esque wig, you will first need to construct a wire frame to support the style. I used white millinery wire, strong white button thread, light colored duct tape, and cheap white nylon netting to construct the frame. Using a frame allows you to create a wig that appears to take up a great deal of space, but makes it much easier for a performer to wear because the wig is mostly hollow and not so heavy.

Figure 10.12 Step 1. Begin by visualizing the overall shape of your wire frame. Have an idea of how tall you wish the frame to be. Cut four pieces of millinery wire a few inches larger than your desired frame height when finished. Turn the end of the wire under to form a loop and bind the loose ends with tape. The loop will keep the frame from poking your performer and give you a place to sew the frame to the wig later. Pin the four pieces of wire onto a canvas head block, forming a square shape around the temples and crown of the head.

Figure 10.13 Step 2. Continue adding pieces of wire as you roughly begin to form the shape of your frame. I find it easier to build up the shape of the frame with small wire pieces. Notice how the wires are placed so that they cross diagonally in places. This adds strength and support to the interior of the frame. Always build with the shape of the end product in mind.

Figure 10.14   Step 3. Where the wires cross, stitch them together with strong thread to hold the wires together.

Figures 10.15 and 10.16   Step 4. Use duct tape to cover where wires are attached on the frame. This will prevent any sharp edges from scratching anyone or anything.

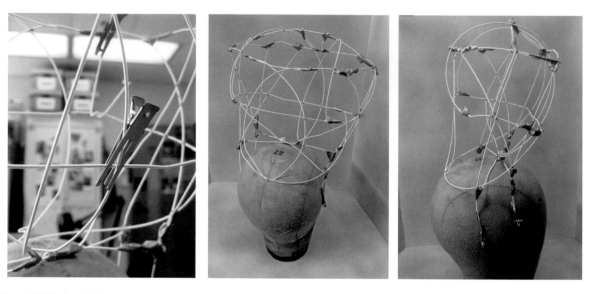

Figure 10.17   Step 5. For easier sewing, use a curl clip to hold the wires together.

Figures 10.18 and 10.19   Step 6. Front and side view of the completed frame shape.

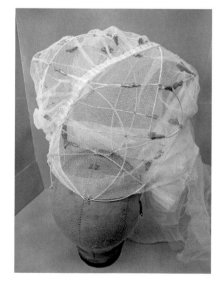

Figure 10.20   Step 7. After tweaking the shape of the wire frame (here, I pinched and tucked the frame to make it slightly shorter), you are ready to cover the frame with nylon netting. I used an old, torn net petticoat, but you can simply buy nylon net yardage from a fabric store. Drape the netting over the frame and neatly gather it until the entire frame is covered.

Figure 10.21   Step 8. Use a curved needle and strong thread to neatly stitch the netting to the wire frame. Do not just stitch the netting around the bottom of the frame—you will need to stitch up the length of all the external wires as well along as the wires that make up the top of the frame. Trim off the excess netting as you work.

Congratulations! Your frame is complete. Set the frame aside for now—you will come back to it when it is time to comb out your set. It is now time to set the wig itself.

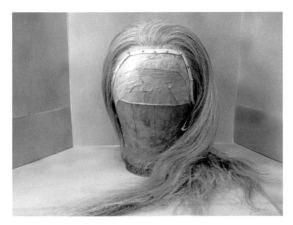

Figure 10.22 Step 9. Begin with a long (at least 16 inches long at the nape of the neck), unlayered wig that has a lot of hair. I chose a wig that was pearly gray in color, but you could use any shade of gray, or you could use a natural color that you add a powdered look to later.

Figure 10.23 Step 10. Set small tendrils of hair going toward the face in front of each ear.

Figure 10.24 Step 11. Use nickel-sized rollers to begin your set. Set the first roller at center front, with a little bit of drag. This will help you to create the slightly concave look in the front of the wig that was part of this period's hair silhouette.

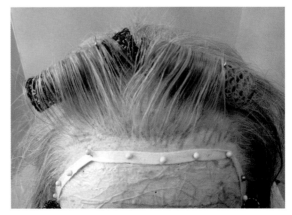

Figure 10.25 Step 12. Continue setting the front section with drag on the rollers.

Figure 10.26   Step 13. The hair on the sides should also be set with drag on the roller, but the roller should now be placed vertically. This will help keep the silhouette close to the head on the sides.

Figure 10.27   Step 14. Continue setting the wig, moving backward on the head. Place the rollers in a brick pattern.

Figure 10.28   Step 15. As you reach the back of the head just below the crown, begin setting the rollers in diagonal rows.

Figure 10.29   Step 16. The next row of diagonal rollers should angle in the opposite direction.

Figures 10.30 and 10.31   Step 17. Set some ringlets of hair at the nape of the neck on dime-sized rollers.

Figure 10.32   Step 18. Continue alternating the direction of the diagonal rows of rollers, working your way down the head toward the nape of the neck.

Figure 10.33   Step 19. At the nape of the neck, set a few more ringlets on dime-sized rollers.

Woman's Georgian/Rococo Wig—The Finished Set

Figures 10.34–38 The finished Georgian/Rococo Woman's style set.

You have now finished setting the wig. Steam the rollers if the wig is made of synthetic hair, or wet the wig thoroughly if it is made of human hair. Place the wig in the wig dryer for at least 75 minutes.

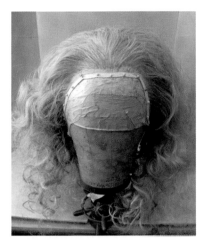

Figure 10.39 Step 20. On another head block, pin some pieces of weft. I like to set extra pieces all around the block, so that I will have extra bits available as I style the wig. Set these on nickel-sized rollers. You will use this hair on the frame of the wig, and wherever you find you need extra coverage in the style. Steam or wet this hair, and dry it alongside the wig.

Figure 10.40 Step 21. Once the extra weft is dry, remove the rollers and brush the hair out with a wide-toothed comb. Stitch the rows of weft on the upper part of the wire frame.

Figure 10.41 Step 22. Remove the rollers from the wig and brush out the hair with a large brush.

Figure 10.42 Step 23. Make a part across the crown of the head, and brush the hair forward towards the hairline.

Figure 10.43 Step 24. Place the wire frame on top of the wig and adjust it until it is sitting in the proper place.

Figure 10.44 Step 25. Use a curved needle and thread to whip stitch the frame in place on the wig.

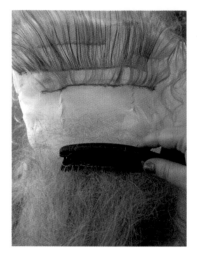

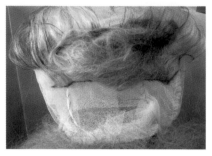

Figure 10.46   Step 27. Pin a hair rat in a matching color to the top of the wire frame. This will add volume and coverage.

Figure 10.45   Step 26. Use a teasing brush to tease the hair at the base of the frame in the front section of the wig.

Figure 10.47   Step 28. Smooth most of the top section of hair up and over the frame.

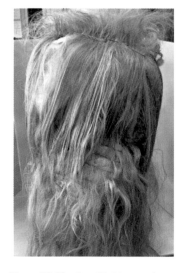

Figure 10.48   Step 29. Pin this hair in place with a combination of bobby pins and hairpins. Mist the hair with hairspray and smooth it with your teasing brush.

Figure 10.49   Step 30. Smooth another section of hair up from the sides of the head, toward the top of the frame. Secure with crossed bobby pins.

Figure 10.50   Step 31. Move to the back of the wig. Tease the hair below the wire frame and mist it with hairspray. Smooth a section of hair up toward the top of the wig. Pin it in place.

Figure 10.51 Step 32. Smooth another section of hair up toward the top of the wig. Mist the section with hairspray, and pin it in place.

Figure 10.52 Step 33. Take another section of hair from the back of the wig, and smooth it up toward the top in a diagonal direction. Do not worry if this hair does not reach all the way to the very top of the wig.

Figure 10.53 Step 34. Cross another section of hair up in the opposite diagonal direction.

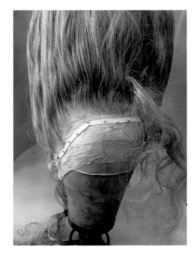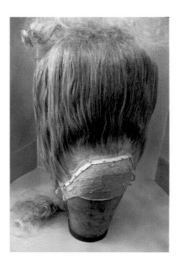

Figure 10.54 Step 35. Leave some hair hanging down at the nape of the neck. This will become long ringlets later.

Figure 10.55 Step 36. Return to the front of the wig, and sweep the remaining hair up to the top of the wire frame.

Figure 10.56 Step 37. All of the hair should now be neatly swept up and all of the flyaway hair should have been smoothed with hairspray and a teasing brush. You should have a cloud of fuzzy curls at the top of the wig and some unfinished curls in the back.

Figure 10.57   Step 38. Use bias tape or ribbon to press some of the wig's waves back into shape. This will add definition and elegance to the style.

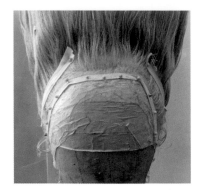

Figure 10.58   Step 39. The bias tape or ribbon should wrap around toward the front of the wig. Mist this hair with hairspray and allow it to set overnight.

Figure 10.59   Step 40. Shape the curls at the top of the wig by brushing them around your finger with a teasing brush. Pin them in place in clusters.

Figure 10.60   Step 41. I used extra pieces of the weft that was curled to add coverage at the sides of the wig. Shape these into long curls by brushing them around a dowel rod.

Figure 10.61   Step 42. I also used extra weft to make cascading curls down the center back of the wig.

Figure 10.62   Step 43. A side view of ringlets added in to cover the sides of the hairstyle. Once the bias tape has been removed from the waves, any remaining gaps in the wig can now be covered in decorations (flowers, jewelry, plumes—whatever suits your design).

Woman's Georgian/Rococo Wig—The Completed Style

Figures 10.63–66 The completed Georgian/Rococo Woman's style. Notice the placement of the decorations throughout the wig style. Photography: Tim Babiak. Model: Ariel Livingston.

Variations

As mentioned earlier in the chapter, variety in this hairstyle can be achieved through hair color. You can use a wig in any shade of gray to mimic the look of powdered hair. You could also use a natural hair color and make it look powdered by dusting it with actual powder, or by misting it lightly with white-colored hairspray. Pastel hairsprays (available at many beauty supply stores) could also be used to achieve that fashionable Easter-egg look. There is almost an infinite number of possible variations in the décor of this era. Illustrations can be found using everything from battleships to stars.

Figure 10.67 Beauty Kampf-Thibodeau chose to decorate her Georgian wig with a bed of roses. Her wig is wider in shape, similar to the hedgehog style, but still has a wire frame underneath for support.

You can also play with the idea of scale. Not every wig for this period has to be of towering height. You can do a smaller version of this hairstyle, which is closer to what Madame Pompadour might have worn in the earlier years of this period.

Figure 10.68 Emma Dirks models a smaller, simpler version of a Georgian hairstyle, styled by Maur Sela.

You can vary your wig's silhouette from this period. Some styles start narrow at the temples and widen as they go higher. Some styles in this period have a rounder silhouette. Still others become almost square at the top. Moreover, the details within these silhouettes can be fun to play with—you can use ringlets, barrel curls, curl clusters, clubbed hair, and draped swags of hair to define your style.

Figure 10.69 Emma Dirks models the wig she styled, which has a rounded silhouette and a natural hair color.

Woman's Hedgehog Wig Styling— Step by Step Instructions

This hairstyle is based on the portrait in Figure 10.6.

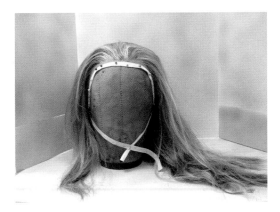

Figure 10.70 Step 1. Begin with a wig that has a lot of short layers (six to eight inches in length) in the front, top, and sides, and is long (at least twelve inches) in the back. I used a synthetic lace front wig. You could also use a shorter layered wig that has had long pieces of weft added to the back.

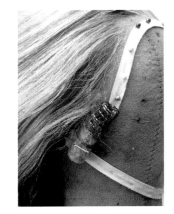

Figure 10.71 Step 2. Set a small tendril of hair over the ear toward the face on a small pencil-sized roller.

Figure 10.72 Step 3. Place the next roller (nickel-sized) at the center front of the wig, and set it at an angle to the face.

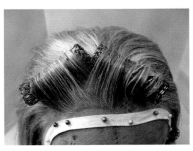

Figure 10.73 Step 4. The next roller should be set at the opposite angle.

Figure 10.74 Step 5. Continue stacking rollers down the side of the hairline. They should be placed almost horizontally.

Figure 10.75   Step 6. Stack rollers horizontally down the other side of the hairline.

Figure 10.76   Step 7. Place a nickel-sized roller behind the first two rollers you set in order to close the gap between the rows of rollers.

Figure 10.77   Step 8. Set a diagonal row of rollers across the back, again bridging the gap between rows of rollers.

Figure 10.78   Step 9. The next row of rollers should be set diagonally in the opposite direction.

Figure 10.79 Step 10. Drop down to dime-sized rollers for the next diagonal row. This will give a little extra curl texture to the back of the head once it is time to style the wig.

Figure 10.80 Step 11. Use nickel-sized rollers for the next diagonal row.

Figure 10.81 Step 12. Use dime-sized rollers to set small sections of hair in sausage curls rolling toward the neck.

Figure 10.82 Step 13. Be sure that you are rolling the sausage curl to be a smooth column of hair by overlapping each turn of hair around the roller.

Figure 10.83 Step 14. Pin the curls at the nape so that the rollers are sitting almost vertically.

Figure 10.84 Step 15. Fill in the rest of the nape of the neck with diagonal rows of rollers, finishing with dime-sized rollers on the bottom.

Woman's Hedgehog Wig—The Finished Set

Figures 10.85–88 The finished Woman's Hedgehog style set.

You have now finished setting the wig. Steam the rollers if the wig is made of synthetic hair, or wet the wig thoroughly if it is made of human hair. Place the wig in the wig dryer for at least 75 minutes.

Figure 10.89 Step 16. Once the wig is dry, begin removing the rollers at the nape of the neck.

Figure 10.90 Step 17. Use a curl clip to separate out the hair that will become the ringlets at the bottom of the hairstyle. This will keep the hair out of the way while you are working on the rest of the style.

Figure 10.91 Step 18. Use a wide-toothed comb to pick through the sections of hair as you remove the rollers.

Figure 10.92 Step 19. After you remove the small roller that was setting the tendril in front of the ear, spritz that section of hair with hairspray.

Figure 10.93 Step 20. The wig, with all rollers removed. All sections of hair have been picked through with a wide-toothed comb.

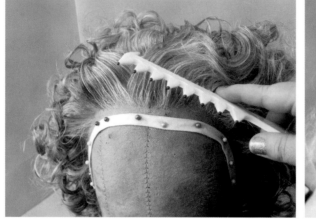 

Figure 10.94   Step 21. Go through the wig a second time with your wide-toothed comb, creating more fluff and volume in the wig.

Figure 10.95   Step 22. Use your smoothing brush to lightly tease the entire wig (except for the ringlets at the bottom). This is the beginning of the cloud of curls you are going to create.

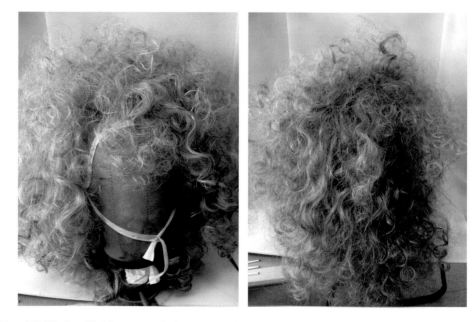

Figures 10.96 and 10.97   Step 23. After teasing the hair, mist it with hairspray. Make sure you are getting the hairspray into the interior of the wig and not just creating a shell around the outside. The best way to do this is to tease a section of hair, then spray it. Repeat this until the whole wig is teased.

Figure 10.98   Step 24. Use your smoothing brush at the center front of the wig to smooth out any roller breaks.

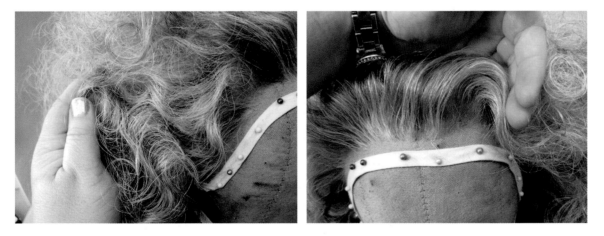

Figures 10.99 and 10.100   Step 25. Use your hands to gently push the waves in place around the face. Once you like their location, mist them with hairspray.

Figure 10.101   Step 26. Clean up the ends of the hair by brushing individual curls around your finger with the smoothing brush.

Figure 10.102   Step 27. Softly gather a cluster of curls in your hand and push them into place. You may need to give the section of hair a half twist.

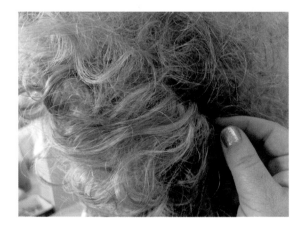

Figure 10.103   Step 28. Pin the section of hair in place with bobby pins. Repeat on the other side of the wig.

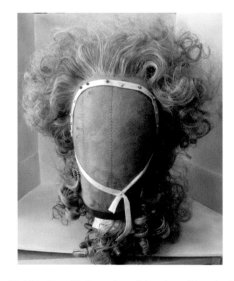

Figure 10.104   Step 29. Front view of the wig at this point in the styling process.

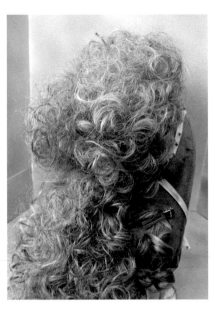

Figure 10.105 Step 30. Continue working your way around the back of the wig by brushing curls around your finger and pinning clusters of curls in place. Be sure to keep the fluffy texture of the hair, and avoid pulling and pinning the hair too tightly.

Figures 10.106 and 10.107 Step 31. At the bottom of the wig, take a section of hair and pin it up diagonally with bobby pins. Repeat on the other side of the wig, crossing the second section of hair over the first.

Figure 10.108   Step 32. Gently pull on the hair to loosen it in order to cover any gaps or holes in the style.

Figure 10.109   Step 33. Use a lifting comb to fluff out the cloud of hair all over the head.

Figures 10.110 and 10.111   Step 34. Return to the sausage curls that you had pinned aside at the nape of the wig. Brush each curl out with your smoothing brush.

Figure 10.112 Step 35. Mist the section of hair with hairspray, and then brush the curl around a dowel rod to shape it. For a fatter curl, lightly tease the inside of the section of hair before brushing it around the rod.

Figure 10.113 Step 36. The completed ringlets.

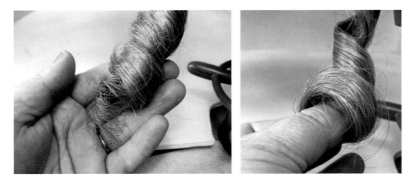

Figures 10.114 and 10.115 Step 37. If the end of the ringlet sticks out, use your finger to push the loose bit up into the body of the curl.

Figure 10.116 Step 38. If you want the finished curl to hang down longer, attach a curl clip to the end of the ringlet and mist with hairspray. The weight of the clip will pull down on the curl to stretch it out. Check on the curl regularly while it is stretching; once it has gotten to the length you want, remove the clip.

Woman's Hedgehog Wig—The Completed Hairstyle

Figures 10.117–120   The completed Woman's Hedgehog style. Photography: Tim Babiak. Model: Ariel Livingston.

Man's Tieback Wig Styling— Step by Step Instructions

This hairstyle contains many elements of the style seen in Figure 10.7, but in a more exaggerated scale inspired by Figure 10.10.

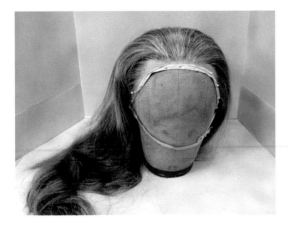

Figure 10.121 Step 1. Begin with a long wig (at least 12 inches long at the nape of the neck). The wig can either have some shorter layers around the front, or be more all one length, as this wig is. This wig is a synthetic hair lace front wig.

Figure 10.122 Step 2. Separate hair out from the center front of the wig for your first roller. Comb it down toward the face, because this roller is going to be set forward of the base so that it poufs out at the roots.

Figure 10.123 Step 3. The finished roller, pinned in position. Notice how it bulges out past the hairline.

Figures 10.124 and 10.125 Step 4. Set several more rollers in the front section of the wig.

Figure 10.126   Step 5. Separate out pieces of hair at the side of the face and secure them with curl clips. Pull the rest of the hair into a low ponytail. Be sure not to pull the ponytail too tight—if it is too tight, the wig may no longer fit the performer.

Figure 10.127   Step 6. Set the hair in the ponytail on dime-sized rollers. As you get to the hair hanging down below the wig block, you will not have anything to pin your roller to. Secure the roller by placing a large hairpin through it—this will keep the roller from coming loose and unrolling.

Figure 10.128   Step 7. Set the side curls on pencil-sized rollers, rolling in an upward direction. (This is one of the few times you will not roll a roller under.) Repeat on the other side of the head.

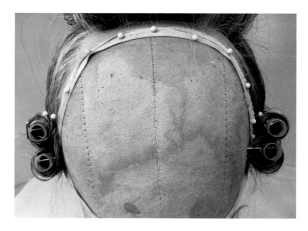

Figure 10.129   Step 8. Check your rollers from the front to be sure that they are even with each other.

Man's Tieback Wig—The Finished Set

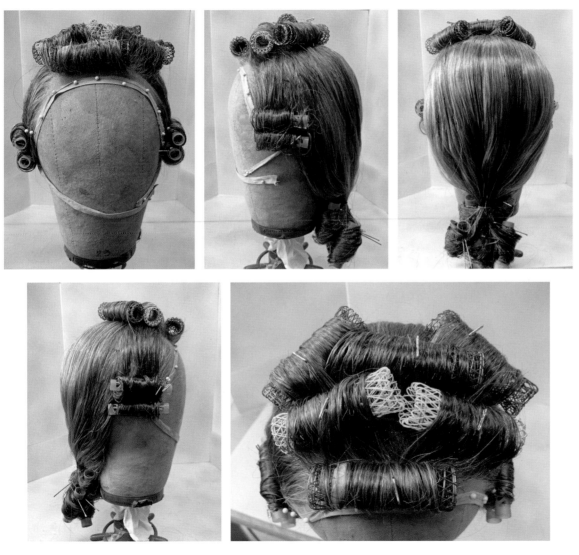

Figures 10.130–134 The finished Men's Tieback style set.

You have now finished setting the wig. Steam the rollers if the wig is made of synthetic hair, or wet the wig thoroughly if it is made of human hair. Place the wig in the wig dryer for at least 75 minutes.

Figure 10.135 Step 9. Once the wig is dry, begin removing the rollers, starting from the bottom of the wig and working your way up toward the front hairline.

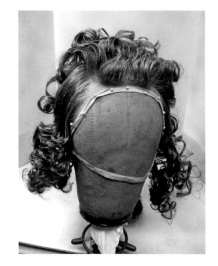

Figure 10.136 Step 10. The wig, with all of the rollers removed.

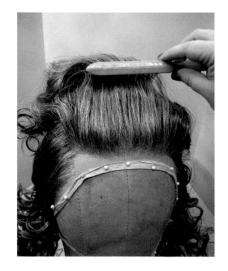

Figure 10.137 Step 11. Use a smoothing brush to brush through the top section of the wig.

Figure 10.138 Step 12. Use your smoothing brush to tease the front section of hair. Remember to mist the hair with hairspray as you work.

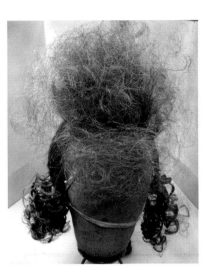

Figure 10.139 Step 13. The teased section of hair will now have quite a lot of height!

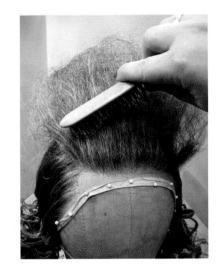

Figure 10.140 Step 14. Use the smoothing brush to begin smoothing the front section.

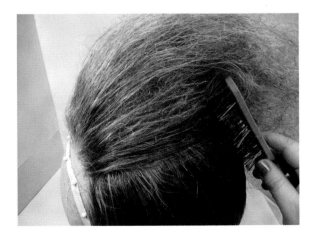

Figure 10.141 Step 15. Smooth the hair around the side so that the front section begins to take on a sort of dome shape.

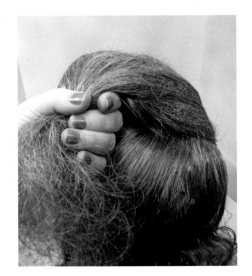

Figure 10.142 Step 16. Gather all of the hair in the section together in your hand.

Figure 10.143 Step 17. Use your fingers to roll the section of hair under, forming a tube of hair.

Figure 10.144 Step 18. Secure the roll of hair with bobby pins.

Figure 10.145 Step 19. Continue smoothing the top section of the hair until it looks neat. Pay special attention to the sides of the dome—use the brush to smooth them down and around the back of the dome.

Figure 10.146 Step 20. Use small hairpins to dress the hair on the sides of the dome.

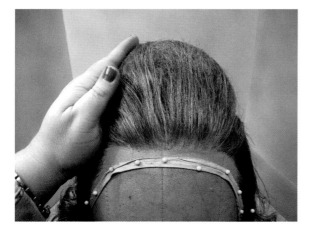

Figure 10.147 Step 21. Use your hands to help pat the wig into the shape you desire.

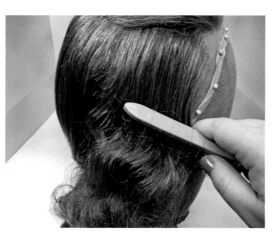

Figure 10.148 Step 22. Move down to the side curls on the wig. Use your smoothing brush to brush through the hair for the top curl.

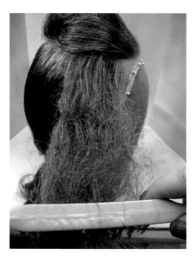

Figure 10.149 Step 23. Lightly tease this section of hair and mist it with hairspray. Use your brush to smooth the underneath section, paying extra attention to the front edge.

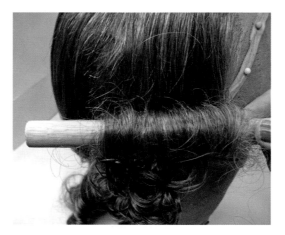

Figure 10.150 Step 24. Use a wooden dowel rod to roll the curl up.

Figure 10.151   Step 25. Once the curl is in the right place, slide the dowel rod out and pin the side curl with bobby pins.

Figure 10.152   Step 26. Use the end of your brush to smooth and tuck in any flyaway hairs.

Figure 10.153   Step 27. Finish the rest of the side curls in the same way. For this wig, there are two side curls on each side. Check from the front to be sure that the curls are symmetrical.

Figure 10.154   Step 28. Use a large brush to brush through the hair in the ponytail.

Figures 10.155 and 10.156 Step 29. Take half of the hair in the ponytail and mist it with hairspray. Brush it around your finger or around a dowel rod to shape the hair into a ringlet.

Figure 10.157 Step 30. The finished curls in the ponytail of the wig.

Figure 10.158 Step 31. The ponytail, or queue, now needs a bow. Bows were most commonly made of grosgrain ribbon, but other kinds of ribbon were used as well. I find it easier to tie the bow first and stitch it to a barrette. This makes a much more attractive and even bow than one made by tying the ribbon around the ponytail.

Figure 10.159 Step 32. The bow is then clipped in place on the back of the wig.

Man's Tieback Wig–The Completed Hairstyle

Figures 10.160–163   The completed Man's Tieback style. Photography: Tim Babiak. Model: Leslie Hethcox.

Variations

A men's tieback wig can be styled to look quite natural, or quite artificial. Exaggerating the height of the front section and increasing the size or number of side curls can make a character seem much more foppish. You can also play with the amount of curls in the ponytail. One single perfect curl in the queue might make the character seem dignified, whereas a clump of many ringlets might make your character seem overly fussy and a slave to fashion. The hair in the queue might be dressed in a club. You can also use a wig bag to create an another alternative look.

Like women's wigs of the period, men's wigs can also be powdered in pastel colors. Play with the texture of the hair to give another indication of character. A tightly curled, frizzy wig often seems like a lower class character than one who is wearing a perfectly smooth wig. Because this period is one when people would have historically been wearing wigs, not their own hair, you can also use hard front wigs to achieve these styles.

Figure 10.164 Philip Weaver models a hard front tieback wig styled by Maur Sela.

eleven

THE REGENCY/EMPIRE PERIOD

{ *1789–1820* }

Figure 11.1   Portrait of Madame Récamier (1777–1849) (oil on canvas), Gerard, Francois Pascal Simon, Baron (1770–1837) / Musée de la
Ville de Paris, Musée Carnavalet, Paris, France / Giraudon / The Bridgeman Art Library International.

Important Events

1789	George Washington becomes the first President of the United States
1795	Directory established to rule France
1795	Pitt's hair powder tax goes into effect
1799	Napoleon overthrows the Directory and establishes the Consulate
1800	Count Alessandro Volta invents the battery
1802	Treaty of Amiens is signed
1804	Napoleon crowns himself Emperor
1804	Lewis and Clark begin their explorations in the western United States
1812	War breaks out between the United States and Britain
1814	Napoleon is exiled to Elba
1815	Napoleon defeated at Waterloo

Important Artists

Jacques-Louis David, François Gerard, Antoine-Jean Gros, Francisco Goya, Jean Baptiste Isabey, Gilbert Stuart.

Important People/Style Icons

Jane Austen, Napoleon and Josephine Bonaparte, Beau Brummell, Lord Byron, Lady Caroline Lamb, Madame Juliette Récamier.

Regency Women

The dramatic events of the French Revolution caused tremendous changes in fashion. It was no longer fashionable to spend lavish amounts of money on powdered wigs and overly embellished clothing. The aesthetic of the time quickly shifted to a simpler ideal of beauty. People looked back to ancient Greece and Rome for their style inspiration. Both genders gave up the idea of wigs and powdered hair and returned to wearing their natural hair. Center parts on women's hairstyles came back into fashion. Soft, styled ringlets framed women's faces. Women also ornamented their hair in a style that imitated the ancient Greeks, often using ribbons or other strips of cloth to bind their hair up at the back.

Figure 11.2 Portrait of Madame Récamier (1777–1849), c. 1798–99 (oil on canvas), Morin, Eulalie (fl. 1798–1800) / Chateau de Versailles, France / The Bridgeman Art Library International. Notice both the center part and the ribbons binding up the hair in this portrait of Madame Récamier.

The knots that the hair was dressed into were called Psyche knots, named after the heroine of a Greek myth. These knots or buns were worn both on top of the head (as in Figure 11.1) and on the back of the head (as in Figure 11.2). Some even more daring women cut their hair short (as in Figure 11.3).

Figure 11.3   *Portrait of Miss Emily Beauchamp with her Pony* (oil on canvas), Opie, John (1761–1807) / Private Collection / The Bridgeman Art Library International. This portrait illustrates one of the daring short hairstyles for women in the Regency period.

One version of this hairstyle was called "hairstyle à la Titus," named after a Roman emperor. The hairstyle had the hair brushed forward from the crown of the head in a way that resembled statues of ancient Roman men. This marked the first time that short hair had been fashionable for women in centuries. Some of society was not ready for such extreme changes and were scandalized by some of the fashion choices being made during this period. After all, going from the Georgian/Rococo period, where the figure was highly corseted and concealed by elaborate gowns and petticoats, and hair was tortured into unnatural shapes and powdered, and moving to a period where the line of the body was visible under clothes and hair was again touchable and moveable was quite an enormous shift. Caricatures of the time mocked and criticized some of these fashion extremes (see Figure 11.4).

Some more conservative women looked to turbans as a fashion accessory (see Figure 11.5). They combined the idea of ancient culture with a hint of ornamentation from the previous era.

Figure 11.4 *Parisian Ladies in their Full Winter Dress for 1800*, an over-the-top exaggerated satirical, November 24, 1799, caricature print by Isaac Cruikshank, on the excesses of the late-1790s Parisian high Greek look, and the too-diaphanous styles allegedly sometimes worn there.

Figure 11.5 Portrait of the Frankland Sisters, 1795, John Hoppner (1758–1810). One of the sisters in the portrait is wearing a turban, fashionable in this era.

Regency Men

In many ways, Regency men had a lot in common with Regency women. They, too, gave up wigs and powdered hair in favor of wearing their natural hair. They also began wearing shorter hair instead of long hair, as many women of the time also did. The most important trendsetter of this era was Beau Brummel (Figure 11.6).

neckcloths and collars that reached all the way up to his chin. His style of dress is sometimes called "dandyism."

Men's hairstyles that swept forward from the crown (see Figure 11.7) were called hairstyles à la Titus (the same name given to the similar women's hairstyle) or hairstyle à la Brutus, named after the Roman assassin of Julius Caesar.

Figure 11.6   George 'Beau' Brummel (1778–1840) (engraving) (b/w photo), English School (19th century) / Private Collection / The Bridgeman Art Library International.

Figure 11.7   *Portrait of a Man*, 1809, Fabre, Francois Xavier (1766–1837) / © National Gallery of Scotland, Edinburgh, Scotland / The Bridgeman Art Library International. The hairstyle in this portrait is an example of a forward swept, Roman-influenced style with accompanying sideburns.

Brummel popularized the fashion of wearing extremely tailored suits and elaborately dressed hair that swept forward from the crown. He also wore the long, curled sideburns that were becoming popular at this time. He was known for wearing high

Some of the men who took the fashions of this time to extremes were called *Incroyables*. These men had the tightest breeches, the highest collars, the tallest hats, and the most elaborately dressed hair.

Regency/Empire Woman's Styling—
Step by Step Instructions

This hairstyle is a combination of the high bun and curls around the face seen in Figure 11.1 and the fuller longer hair over the ears seen in Figure 11.5.

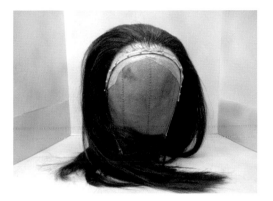

Figure 11.8 Step 1. Begin with a wig that is mostly long (ten to twele inches at the nape of the neck), with shorter layers (four to eight inches) around the face. This wig is a synthetic lace front wig.

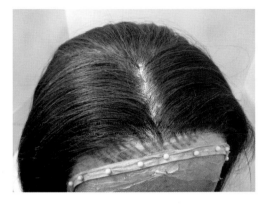

Figure 11.9 Step 2. Make a center part in the front section of the wig.

Figure 11.10 Step 3. Separate out the hair on either side of the center part in front of the ears. Pull most of the remaining hair into a ponytail at the crown of the head.

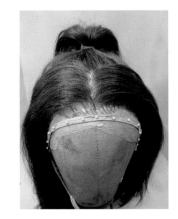

Figure 11.11 Step 4. Front view of the ponytail placement and the front sections of the hair in front of the ears.

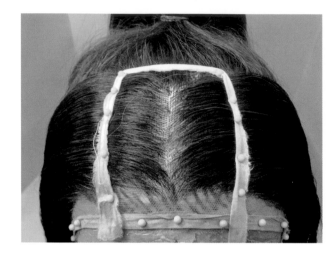

Figure 11.12 Step 5. Use a piece of bias tape or twill tape and pin it in place to hold the top few inches of hair on either side of the part flat and smooth.

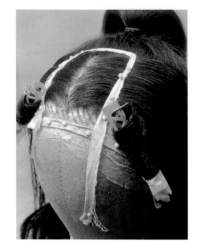

Figure 11.13 Step 6. Begin rolling small sections of hair toward the face on pencil-sized rollers.

Figure 11.14 Step 7. Continue rolling small sections of hair toward the face, increasing the size of the rollers to dime-sized as you work toward the back of the section of hair.

Figure 11.15 Step 8. The first row of rollers on both sides, completed.

Figure 11.16 Step 9. On the next row down, set two pencil-sized rollers going toward the face, and one slightly larger roller directing away from the face.

Figure 11.17 Step 10. Use nickel-sized rollers to set the remaining hair going away from the face. This should include the hair behind the ears.

Figure 11.18 Step 11. Set any small tendrils of hair at the nape of the neck on perm rods rolling toward the nape of the neck. This will help conceal the back edge of the wig.

Figure 11.19 Step 12. Move to the ponytail at the crown of the head. Set the ponytail on dime-sized rollers that radiate away from the center of the ponytail.

Figure 11.20   Step 13. The finished ponytail, with all the hair set in rollers.

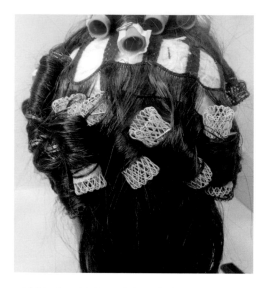

Figure 11.21   Step 14. Use nickel-sized rollers to set the remaining hair in the back of the wig in alternating diagonal rows.

Figure 11.22   Step 15. The very last row of the wig has been set on dime-sized rollers.

Regency Woman's Hairstyle—The Finished Set

Figures 11.23–26 The finished Regency/Empire Woman's style set.

Once you have finished setting the wig, steam each roller thoroughly if the wig is made of synthetic hair. If the wig is human hair, soak each roller with water from a spray bottle. After steaming or wetting, place the wig in a wig dryer for 75 minutes.

To style:

Figure 11.27   Step 16. Begin removing the rollers from the back nape section of the wig.

Figure 11.28   Step 17. Carefully unwind the small rollers set in the front section of hair in front of the ears.

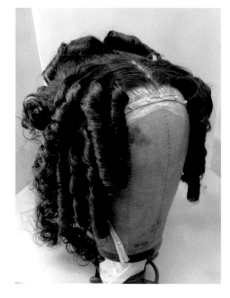

Figure 11.29   Step 18. The wig, after all of the rollers have been removed.

Figure 11.30   Step 19. Use a large brush to brush through the hair in both the back section of the wig and in the ponytail.

Figure 11.31 Step 20. The hair in the back, brushed through. Using a large brush helps eliminate roller breaks in the finished hairstyle.

Figure 11.32 Step 21. Use a duckbill clip to secure the hair in the ponytail up and out of the way for now.

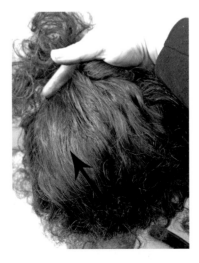

Figure 11.33 Step 22. Divide the hair hanging down in the back in half. Pull half of this hair up toward the base of the ponytail and secure with bobby pins.

Figure 11.34 Step 23. Pull the other half of the hair diagonally up toward the opposite side of the base of the ponytail and secure the section with bobby pins. Spritz the pinned section of hair with hairspray and use a smoothing brush to control any flyaway hairs.

Figure 11.35   Step 24. Take the section of hair from the front section of hair that was set on nickel-sized rollers. Smooth this hair back and use bobby pins to pin it at the base of the ponytail.

Figure 11.36   Step 25. Undo the duckbill clip that was holding the hair in the ponytail away from the back. Make the hair in the ponytail and the other section of hair that was pinned at the base of the ponytail into a high bun. Begin by brushing sections of hair around two fingers, using a smoothing brush.

Figure 11.37   Step 26. Use bobby pins to secure each curl in place. You should not pin each curl in a perfect roll. Create variety in the bun by pulling and twisting some of the rolls you create by brushing the sections around your fingers.

Figure 11.38   Step 27. Continue working your way around the bun, creating a cluster of curls.

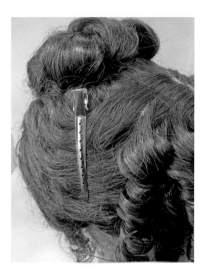

Figure 11.39 Step 28. If the back section of hair looks too bulky or wide, use a duckbill clip to flatten the hair in place.

Figure 11.40 Step 29. Move to the front section of hair. Use a smoothing brush to brush through this section of hair.

Figure 11.41 Step 30. Use a smoothing brush to form the hair into neat ringlets around one finger. You can also smooth the hair around a small dowel rod.

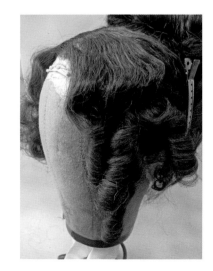

Figure 11.42 Step 31. All of the hair in front of the ears has been shaped into ringlets.

Figure 11.43 Step 32. If you wish for the ringlets to be longer, place a small curl clip at the bottom to weight the curl down and spritz the curl lightly with hairspray. Check the curl periodically (I usually check about every 30 minutes) until it has stretched to the desired length.

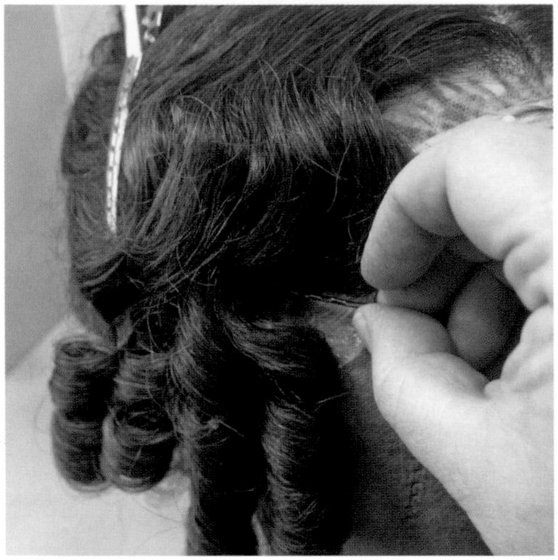

Figure 11.44 Step 33. Use a bobby pin to secure the front ringlets so that they do not bounce around too much.

Figure 11.45 Step 34. Pin a hairnet over the bun so that it stays looking neat. This is especially important if the wig is going to be worn with a bonnet or turban.

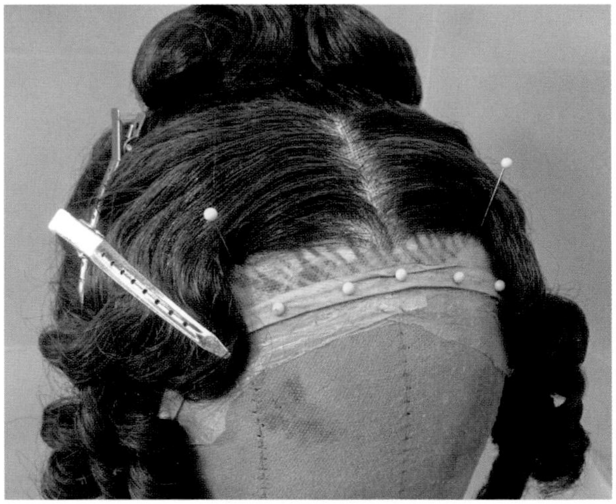

Figure 11.46 Step 35. Use a duckbill clip to flatten the waves at the front of the head. This will help to make a nice transition from the flat section at the top of the head to the ringlets.

Regency Woman—The Completed Hairstyle

Figures 11.47–50　The completed Regency/Empire Woman's style. Photography: Tim Babiak. Model: Ivy Negron.

Variations

You can create variety in your Regency hairstyles by moving the placement of the bun. For example, in Figure 11.51, the woman's bun is just beneath the crown of her head.

Figure 11.51   Self-portrait of Rolinda Sharples, with her mother Ellen Sharples, 1820.

The bun in Figure 11.52 has been styled much higher, directly on the crown of the head.

Figure 11.52   Regency wig styled by Maur Sela, modeled by Lexi O'Reilly.

You can experiment with the length of the ringlets around the face—some wigs could be styled with shorter ringlets, some with longer ringlets. You can also vary the amount of ringlets, with some of your wigs having only one or two, and others having a clump of them. Turbans could be added to some hairstyles, and some could be dressed with ribbons and cords in order to reflect the classical influences of the period.

Figure 11.53   The Empress Josephine, by Andrea Appiani, 1808. In this portrait of Josephine Bonaparte, her hair has been dressed in a very Grecian manner, including Grecian-influenced decorations and some ringlets hanging down the nape of her neck.

twelve

THE BIEDERMEIER PERIOD

{ *1820–1835* }

Figure 12.1 *Newest Fashions for January 1831*, Fashionable Head-dresses from Vol. VIII of The World of Fashion and Continental Fenilletons, pub. 1831 (engraving), English School (19th century) / © Central Saint Martins College of Art and Design, London / The Bridgeman Art Library.

Biedermeier Women

The term "biedermeier" refers to an art and aesthetic movement and era where the focus was on a new urban middle class. The movement began with an emphasis on clean lines and little ornamentation, but as time passed, the middle class became interested in displaying more of their wealth. This led to a greater use of ornament and decoration, which also translated to the fashion and hairstyles of the time. Women's hair was parted either in the center, or parted in a "V" shape. The hair on the top of the head was usually very flat to the head. The hair was dressed in elaborate bunches of curls around the sides of the face (see Figure 12.2).

Important Events

1821	Napoleon I dies in exile
1824	Ludwig van Beethoven's *Symphony No. 9* premieres in Vienna
1825	The Erie Canal is completed
1826	Nicèphore Nièpce creates a true photograph
1830	The Baltimore and Ohio railroad opens in the United States
1831	Nat Turner's Rebellion
1831–36	Charles Darwin is a part of the second voyage of the *IIMS Beagle*, on which he collects information that will lead to his theory of evolution
1833	Richard Wagner composes his first opera, *Die Feen*
1836	Charles Dickens publishes *The Pickwick Papers*, his first novel

Important Artists/Designers

William Blake, Alexander Briullov, John Constable, Eugen Delacroix, Ferdinand Georg Waldmuller.

Important People/Style Icons

Ludwig van Beethoven, Duchesse de Berry, Johann Wolfgang von Goethe, Princess Maria Christina of Naples and Sicily, Princess Marie-Carolina of Austria, Maria Theresa of Austria, Edgar Allan Poe, Victoria Duchess of Kent.

Figure 12.2 Portrait of a young woman, c. 1833–34 (oil on canvas), Schwiter, Ludwig August or Louis August (1805–89) / Musée des Beaux-Arts, Orléans, France / Giraudon / The Bridgeman Art Library. This woman wears a typical day look of the Biedermeier period.

For daytime, the remaining hair was usually dressed on the very top of the head in simple braids and loops. Sometimes there were also braids looped next to the face instead of bunches of curls, as in Figure 12.3.

Figure 12.3 Caroline, Countess of Holnstein, 1834, Joseph Karl Stieler. The countess wears a braided version of a Biedermeier hairstyle.

(Bonnets were very fashionable for daytime, so the hairstyles had to remain fairly simple so they would fit underneath the bonnets.) In the back, these hairstyles were usually pulled up very close to the head and tucked into a neat twist. This helped show off the long necks and delicate shoulders exposed by the fashionable wide-sleeved gowns of this time.

Hairstyles for evening featured very tall, ornamented loops and braids of hair. These tall structures were likely an artificial piece of hair that was added to the crown of the head in order to augment a woman's hairstyle. These elaborate hairstyles were often called Apollo Knots, because they were thought to be very Greek in influence. Examples of the great variety of Apollo Knots can be seen in Figure 12.1. These hairstyles reflected the airy aesthetic of this era and was decorated with flowers, plumes, and ribbons.

Biedermeier Men

Men's hairstyles during this period were growing longer in length and becoming fuller. Side parts were becoming quite fashionable, as in Figure 12.4.

Figure 12.4   Portrait of Antoine Julien Meffre-Rouzan, 1833, Eugène François Marie-Joseph Devéria. This gentleman wears his hair in a style that is wider on the sides over the ears and has a fashionable side part.

Men were also growing their sideburns longer and curling them more elaborately (see Figure 12.5).

Figure 12.5   *The Bride*, c. 1820 (litho), Boilly, Louis Leopold (1761–1845) / Private Collection / The Bridgeman Art Library. The gentleman in the lower left of this lithograph wears carefully tousled hair and longer, more elaborate sideburns. The women show a variety of daytime hairstyles from this period.

Mustaches for men, such as the one worn in Figure 12.4, were still in fashion.

Woman's Biedermeier/Apollo Knot Styling— Step by Step Instructions

This look is based on the styles in Figure 12.1.

Figure 12.6 Step 1. Begin with a long wig that has shorter layers (four to six inches long) around the face, if possible. The back should be long enough (twelve inches from the nape) to at least pull up into a French twist. Here, I have used a synthetic lace front wig. You may also need to add a switch or ponytail of hair in a matching color. Here, I used both a switch and a small braided piece.

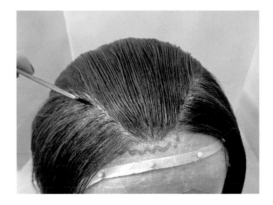

Figure 12.7 Step 2. Make a clean, "V"-shaped part in the front section of the wig.

Figure 12.8 Step 3. Pull the hair in the "V"-shaped section back into a ponytail that sits right at the crown of the head.

Figure 12.9 Step 4. To create the side bunches of curls, set the wig on pencil-sized rollers on both sides. Note: unlike most roller setting, you are going to set these pencil rollers by rolling them up, instead of rolling them down and under.

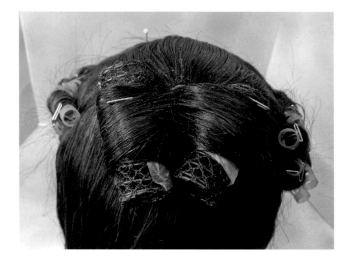

Figure 12.10   Step 5. Set the hair in the crown ponytail in two quarter-sized rollers.

Figure 12.11   Step 6. Begin setting the outside edges of the back of the wig on quarter-sized rollers. Roll these so that they are rolling toward the center of the head.

Figure 12.12   Step 7. Set the hair below the crown ponytail rolling down toward the nape on quarter-sized rollers in alternating diagonal rows.

Figure 12.13   Step 8. Finish setting the hair at the nape of the wig on half-dollar-sized rollers.

Biedermeier Woman's Hairstyle—The Finished Set

Figures 12.14–17 The finished Biedermeier/Apollo Knot Woman's style set.

Once you have finished setting the wig, steam each roller thoroughly if the wig is made of synthetic hair. If the wig is human hair, soak each roller with water from a spray bottle. After steaming or wetting, place the wig in a wig dryer for 75 minutes. While the wig is drying, you can construct the support loops that this hairstyle will require.

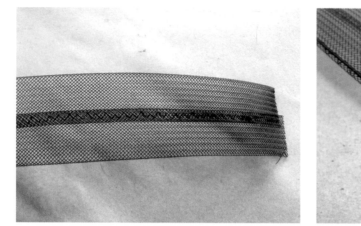

Figure 12.18   Step 9. Begin by zigzag stitching two pieces of one-inch wide horsehair together on a sewing machine. (If you do not have access to a sewing machine, you can stitch these together by hand.) You should use a color of horsehair that matches the wig. Horsehair can also be sprayed with craft spray if you need to change the color.

Figure 12.19   Step 10. Whip stitch millinery wire along each side of the horsehair piece. Finish off the end by folding up the horsehair and stitching it so that it forms a loop. If you do not have millinery wire, heavy floral wire can be substituted. Make sure that you turn up the ends of the wire so that they are not poking out where they can scratch the performer or snag the wig.

Figure 12.20   Step 11. Fold the piece of wired horsehair in half in order to create a loop. Stitch the ends together to create the finished loop. For this style, you will need to create two loops, with one being slightly shorter than the other. You will need to create one horsehair base for each loop you wish to incorporate in the finished style.

To style the wig:

Figure 12.21 Step 12. Remove all of the rollers from the wig, beginning at the nape of the neck and working up. Brush out the hair in the back with a large brush.

Figure 12.22 Step 13. Make a French twist in the back of the wig (see Chapter 1 for basic French twist instructions). Twist the hair and pin it up going toward the crown of the head. Make sure to pin into the first row of bobby pins you put down in order to make the twist extra secure. Leave the ends of the hair loose at the crown of the head for now.

Figure 12.23 Step 14. Move to the front of the wig. Shape the side bunches of curls by brushing each curl around your finger and pinning it in place with a bobby pin.

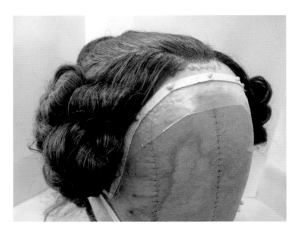

Figure 12.24 Step 15. A finished view of the side curls.

Figure 12.25   Step 16. Pin the support loops at the crown of the wig just above where the French twist ends. Arrange them in the shape you want. Make sure they are securely anchored with crossed bobby pins at the base.

Figure 12.26   Step 17. Sweep the hair in the small crown ponytail over the shorter support loop. Mist the section of hair with hairspray and smooth it over the loop as you work.

Figure 12.27   Step 18. Wrap the ends of the hair around the base of the support loop.

Figure 12.28   Step 19. Secure the ponytail switch at the base of the support loops with bobby pins.

Figure 12.29   Step 20. Sweep the hair from the switch up and over the taller support loop. Again, spray with hairspray and smooth the hair as you work. You may need to slide in some concealed bobby pins in order to secure the underlayer of hair to the wired loop. If you have extra hair length at the end of the switch, wrap it around the support base.

Figure 12.30   Step 21. Attach the small braided piece at the base of the taller support loop.

Figures 12.31 and 12.32   Step 22. Arrange the braid up and around the loops in a way that looks pretty.

Figure 12.33   Step 23. Front view of the finished loops and braid.

Figure 12.34   Step 24. Take the hair left from the French twist and divide in half. Sweep half of the hair around the support bases going toward the left side of the head, and half of the hair around the bases going toward the right side of the head.

Figure 12.35   Step 25. Add decorations to the wig.

Figure 12.36   Step 26. You may need to wrap the finishing hair around the base after the decorations are in place. This could help hold the décor more securely.

Figure 12.37   Step 27. Finish off the ends of the hair around the base by forming them into a small loop or curl, and pin in place.

Woman's Biedermeier/Apollo Knot—The Completed Hairstyle

Figures 12.38–41   The completed Biedermeier/Apollo Knot Woman's style. Photography: Tim Babiak. Model: Josephine McAdam.

Variations

To create variety, you can use both the looks with bunches of curls at the sides of the face (such as in Figures 12.1 and 12.2) and with the braids on the side of the face (such as in Figure 12.3). You might choose to create a combination of simpler daytime hairstyles and more elaborate evening hairstyles. You can also use a vast array of different decorative elements to create some truly unique looks.

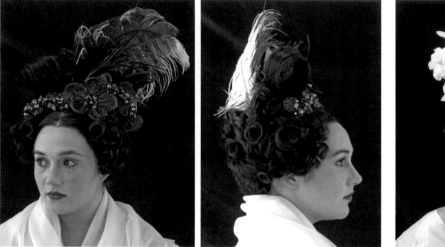

Figures 12.42 and 12.43 Thumper Gosney has decorated her Biedermeier wig with feather plumes and an ornate jeweled band.

Figure 12.44 Kara Meche has accented her 1830s look with a veritable garden of flowers.

Glossary of Hairstyling Terms

AFRO—a hairstyle, originating on people of African descent, in which naturally curly hair is allowed to grow and become bushy in a round fashion on the head.

AGGRAVATORS—short men's curls, seen in the nineteenth century, that were combed right to the outer corner of each eye.

ALEXANDRA CURL—a long spiral curl that is usually worn behind one ear.

ALLONGE—a long curly men's wig, worn during the Restoration period, that is styled in high curls above the forehead.

APOLLO KNOT—a piece made of artificial hair that is looped, coiled, and stiffened to stand up on the crown of the head as part of a popular hairstyle of the 1830s.

BAG WIG—an eighteenth-century wig where the hair in the back is contained in a fabric bag.

BANDEAU—an artificial hairpiece that was worn on the front of the head and secured at the nape of the neck with a ribbon. A bandeau could be styled in a variety of ways. It is similar to a **transformation**.

BANGS—a fringe of hair, usually brushed forward onto the forehead.

BAROQUE—a style characterized by extravagant ornament and detail.

BARREL CURL—a hollow curl that is rolled up on itself and pinned in place. This was very commonly seen on wigs in the mid to late eighteenth century.

BARRISTER'S WIG—the traditional wig worn by barristers in British courts. The wig consists of frizzy loops on top, rows of barrel curls, and two tails with tiny curls at the bottom.

BASIN OR BOWL CUT—any haircut where a bowl or basin is placed on the head and the hair is cut to the edges of the bowl. It appears in nearly all ages of history.

BEATLE CUT/MOP TOP—a hairstyle popularized in the 1960s by the Beatles. The style consisted of hair that was brushed forward onto the forehead and roughly the same length all around the head. This hairstyle was considered radical because of its length after the very short men's haircuts of the 1950s.

BEEHIVE—a 1960s' hairdo where the hair is pulled on top of the head, teased, and smoothed into a dome that resembles a beehive.

BOB—a short hairstyle for women, popularized in the 1920s, where the hair was chopped off at chin level. The bob has continued its popularity to the present day, where many different variations of the bob have been created.

BOB WIG—a seventeenth- and eighteenth-century wig with short curls at the bottom. There was both a long bob wig and a short bob wig. These wigs were most frequently worn by laborers and tradesmen.

BOUFFANT—any hairstyle that is teased around the face for volume.

BRAID—a length of hair where the strands are woven or twisted together. Three sections of hair are used to make the most common braid, but braids can be made with many more sections.

BRUTUS STYLE—a short tousled hairstyle popularized by French Revolutionaries.

BUN—any tightly wound arrangement (usually circular in shape) of hair on the back of the head.

BUZZ CUT—also called a crew cut, this is a haircut where the hair is shaved evenly around the head, at a short length very close to the scalp.

CADOGAN/CLUB—a knot of hair at the nape of the neck that was folded back onto itself and tied around the middle. This was a popular style in the late eighteenth century.

CAESAR HAIRCUT—a short layered men's haircut with short bangs that are brushed onto the face.

CAGE—a wire frame used to support large, structural hairstyles.

CASCADE—an artificial hairpiece with long falling curls.

CAULIFLOWER WIG—a short, white, curled bob wig that was worn by clergymen and physicians in the eighteenth century.

CHIGNON—a smooth twist, knot, or roll of hair, worn on the back of the head.

CHONMAGE—a traditional Japanese men's hairstyle where the top of the head is either shaved or slicked down; the rest of the hair is pulled into a small ponytail and folded up onto the crown of the head.

CLUB—see **Cadogan**.

COIF—can refer to either a close-fitting cap, or the act of creating a hairstyle.

COIL—a type of bun where the hair is wound in concentric circles and pinned.

CORNROWS—a type of braid where a narrow strip of hair is braided tightly against the scalp.

CORONET—a hairstyle that mimics a crown, usually consisting of braids wrapped around the head.

COXCOMB—a hairstyle where the hair at the center of the forehead is swept up and back into a curl. This hairstyle got its name from its resemblance to the crest of a rooster.

CRESPINE—a jeweled net for securing the hair, used in the fifteenth century.

CRIMPING—the act of pressing hair between shaped metal plates to create texture.

CYPRIOTE CURL—a sculptural curl that was piled onto a frame around the face in some Roman women's hairstyles.

DREADLOCK—a hairstyle that forms over time when naturally curly hair is allowed to wind around itself, eventually forming a solid lock of hair.

DUCKTAIL—a men's haircut, popular in the 1950s, where the hair was parted in the center back like a duck's tail. The hair on the sides was combed back and the hair in the front was intentionally disarrayed so that some pieces hung down.

FADE—a haircut, commonly worn by black men, where the hair tapers from very short to almost non-existent.

FALL—a hairpiece used to add thickness and length to the back of the head. It generally sits at the top of the head and covers to the nape of the neck.

FAVORITES—locks of curly hair that dangle at the temples.

FEATHERED HAIR—a haircut where the layers are tapered, especially around the face. This hairstyle was very popular in the 1970s.

FINGER WAVE—a method of setting wave into hair by using the fingers to mold the waves in place.

FLAT TOP—a haircut that is similar to a crew cut, except the hair is cut into a flat plane on top.

FLIP—a hairstyle where the bottom ends are curled or flipped up. A popular hairstyle in the 1960s.

FONTANGE—a women's hairstyle of the Restoration period where the hair over the forehead is dressed in wired curls. This was often topped by the Fontange headdress which was made of stiffened, pleated lace. This hairstyle is named after the Duchesse de Fontanges, who created the style after her original hairstyle fell down. She tied her hair up off her forehead with a ribbon garter, and the hairstyle caught on after Louis XIV admired it on her.

FRENCH BRAID—a method of braiding where hair is gradually added to the braid in sections, instead of braiding all of the hair together at once. This allows the braid to lie extremely close to the head.

FRENCH DOT—a tiny goatee that sits directly under the bottom lip.

FRENCH ROLL—a hairstyle where the hair is arranged in a vertical roll on the back of the head. Also called a French twist.

FRENCH TWIST—see **French roll**.

FRINGE—short hair brushed forward. Fringe is sometimes used as another word for bangs.

FRISETTE—a fringe of curled or frizzed hair worn off the forehead. Usually an artificial piece.

FRIZZLE—a short, crisp curl.

FULL BOTTOM WIG—a type of wig, popular in the eighteenth century, which was very large and elaborately curled, with a section of curls falling in front of each shoulder.

GORDIAN KNOT—an intricate, figure-of-eight knot of hair.

GRECIAN KNOT—a style where the hair at the nape of the neck was coiled and knotted to resemble the hairstyle of ancient Greek women.

HANDLEBAR MUSTACHE—a mustache style where the ends stick out past the lips and turn up at the ends. These ends are often waxed into points.

HEDGEHOG—a name for hairstyles worn by both men and women in the late eighteenth century. For men, this was a hairstyle where the hair was short all around the face and worn spiked out. For women, the hedgehog hairstyle consisted of a shorter cloud of curls around the face, with long ringlets hanging down in the back.

HIME CUT—an Asian hairstyle that consists of long straight hair with blunt bangs and a section of hair that is cut to shoulder length.

HOLLYWOOD BEARD—a short full beard where the section of hair under the lower lip and on the front of the chin area has been shaved away.

HURLUBERLU—a women's hairstyle of the late seventeenth century, where the hair is usually center parted, and worn very curly all around the head, with a few long ringlets hanging down the back. The term roughly translates from the French to "screwball," "cabbage head," or "scatter brain."

KISS CURL/SPIT CURL—a small short curl that is worn curling onto the face.

LADYKILLER—also referred to as Dundreary whiskers or Piccadilly Weepers. Long, drooping sideburns that nearly touch the shoulders.

LAPPET—a longer curl that hangs loose on the face or neck.

LIBERTY SPIKES—a hairstyle popularized by the British punk culture of the 1970s where the hair was styled into a wide pointed spike that stuck out all over the head. This hairstyle often requires the use of extreme styling products, including glue, egg whites, gelatin, starch, and hairspray, in order to keep its stiff shape.

LION WIG—the term can either refer to an eighteenth-century wig that resembles the mane of a lion, or, more commonly, a style of Kabuki wig. A lion Kabuki wig is usually white in color and consists of long bangs brushed forward onto the forehead and three long full tails of hair (one over each shoulder and one hanging down the back).

LOCK OF HORUS—a lock of hair that was left uncut over the right ear of young Egyptian boys. (The rest of the head was shaved.)

LOVELOCK—a long curl or ringlet of hair that is pulled forward to hang over the shoulder. These were worn by both men and women in the Cavalier period.

MACARONI—a male dandy or fop of the late eighteenth century. The term *macaroni* also refers to the wig style worn by these dandies where the hair in the front was dressed very tall and sometimes pointy. A small hat was often perched on this tall section of hair. The hair in the back of this wig style was usually pulled into a queue and clubbed.

MARCEL WAVE—a method of waving the hair where the hair was pressed with hot waving irons. It is a similar method of hairstyling to crimping the hair. It was invented by French hairdresser Marcel Grateau in 1872.

MOHAWK—a hairstyle where the entire head is shaved to the skin except for a strip of hair down the center that is spiked up.

MOMOWARE—a Japanese hairstyle worn by maiko (apprentice geisha). This style is known as the "divided peach."

MULLET—a hairstyle where the hair is cut short in the front and sides and left long in the back.

MUTTON CHOP—a type of sideburn that is narrow near the temple and wide at the jaw line.

ODANGO—a hairstyle, inspired by Japanese anime, where the hair is arranged in two buns on top of the head that resemble animal ears.

PAGEBOY—a long bobbed hairstyle, usually just touching the shoulders, with the ends turned under. This hairstyle first came into being as a style used on medieval boys serving under knights. It later gained popularity as a women's hairstyle in the 1930s and 40s.

PENCIL MUSTACHE—a mustache made up of a very thin line of hairs.

PERIWIG—another term for a wig from the seventeenth century, especially used by the British.

PERM—a slang term for a permanent wave. This is a process where the hair is rolled onto tiny rollers and treated with chemicals so that the hair takes on a "permanent" curl.

PERRUKE/PERRUQUE—the French word for wig.

PIGTAIL—long hair that is pulled back, cinched, and braided.

PIGTAIL WIG—a men's wig with a long queue that is bound all the way to the tip by a ribbon.

PIN CURL—a flat curl held in place by a hairpin while it is being set.

PIXIE CUT—a short women's hairstyle that has wispy layered bangs.

PLAIT—another word for braid. There are many varieties of plaits.

POMPADOUR—a hairstyle where the hair is not parted, and is brushed straight back off of the forehead with some height. Originally named for Madame de Pompadour. This term later became associated with a men's hairstyle in the 1950s where the hair above the forehead was styled extremely high and pouffed.

PONYTAIL—long hair that is pulled close to the head, cinched, and allowed to hang loose.

PSYCHE KNOT—a style where the hair is divided into two sections. The two sections are coiled and one coiled is pulled through the center of the other coil. This knot is usually placed on the back of the head just below the crown.

QUEUE—a long tail of hair, usually referring to a men's hairstyle. A queue can be curled or braided.

QUIFF—a hairstyle, similar to the pompadour, where the hair over the forehead is shaped into a sculpted curl or wave.

RAT TAIL—a small section of hair, usually at the nape of the neck, which is allowed to grow much longer than the rest of the hair.

RINGLET—any long, vertical hanging curl.

ROUNDHEAD—a name applied to the Puritans who supported Parliament against Charles I in England. The name came from their rounded bowl cuts.

SAUSAGE CURL—a long vertical curl that has an uninterrupted tube shape.

SHAG—a hairstyle where all of the hair is cut into layers of various lengths. This style was first popularized in the 1970s.

SHAITTEL/SHEITEL—the Yiddish word for the wigs worn by married Orthodox Jewish women. These wigs allow the women to follow the Jewish law requiring them to keep their hair/head covered.

SHIMADA—a Japanese women's hairstyle, usually worn by geisha.

SHINGLE—a version of the 1920s' bob haircut where the hair was cut to the occipital bone; the hair remaining underneath was cut into a V shape.

SIDEBURN—a short side whisker, worn without a beard. The style was named for the American Civil War general Ambrose Burnside.

SNOOD—an ornamental net that holds or contains part of the hair.

SPADE BEARD—a beard that is cut into a rounded or pointed blade shape.

TENDRIL—a small wisp of curly hair, usually found in front of the ear.

TIEBACK—another term for a man's eighteenth-century wig that was pulled back into a queue.

TITUS—a short layered women's hairstyle seen in the nineteenth century. This was one of the rare instances of a short women's hairstyle before the twentieth century.

TONSURE—a hairstyle seen on monks where the hair at the crown of the head is shaved.

TRANSFORMATION—an artificial hairpiece that goes all the way around the head, but does not have a crown.

UPDO—any hairstyle where all of the hair is pulled up and away from the neck.

VAN DYCK BEARD—a small pointed goatee. The style gets its name from the beards that frequently appeared in the portraits painted by Sir Anthony Van Dyck.

VICTORY ROLL—a 1940s hairstyle where the hair on the sides of the head is swept up into hollow rolls and pinned. A true victory roll has the rolls going all the way down the head until they meet in a point at the nape of the neck, forming a V for Victory.

WALRUS MUSTACHE—a large mustache that hangs over the lips and drops down at the outer corners of the mouth.

WEDGE—a haircut, popularized in the 1970s, which uses a weight line and tapered layer to create the illusion of extra fullness. This is sometimes referred to as a stacked haircut.

ZULU KNOT—an African hairstyle where the hair is divided in triangular or rectangular sections and each section is tightly twisted into a knot.

List of Historical Films Set in Each Era: Ancient Egypt–1830s

These films can be used as a good reference for the periods in question. Primary research is direct research from a historical period, and is always the most authentic reference and the one you should look to first. Primary research materials include actual wigs from the period (very rare due to their rapid deterioration), portraits painted during a period, and photographs. Interpretations of other time periods, including films, constitute secondary research. Keep in mind that the look of a film is always visually affected by the year the film was made, so while the looks portrayed in the film may not be 100 percent authentic, they are still great for giving you a feel for the period and a place from which to begin brainstorming ideas and inspiring your research. There is no substitute for authentic period research, but these films make for excellent supplementary material.

The Ancient Egyptian Era

Cleopatra (1934 and 1963)
The Scorpion King (2002)
The Ten Commandments (1956)

The Ancient Greece Era

300 (2007)
Clash of the Titans (1981 and 2010)
Immortals (2011)
The Trojan Women (1971)
Troy (2004)

The Ancient Roman Era

Ben Hur (1959)
Caligula (1979)
Gladiator (2000)
I, Claudius (1976)
Spartacus (1960 and 2004)

The Middle Ages

Braveheart (1995)
King Arthur (2004)
Kingdom of Heaven (2005)
The Lion in Winter (1968 and 2003)
Tristan and Isolde (2006)

The Renaissance Era

The Agony and the Ecstasy (1965)
Black Arrow (1985)
Ever After (1998)
The Other Boleyn Girl (2008)
Romeo and Juliet (1968)

The Elizabethan Era

Elizabeth (1998)
Elizabeth: the Golden Age (2007)
Lady Jane (1986)
The New World (2005)
Shakespeare in Love (1998)

The Cavalier/Jacobean Period

Cyrano de Bergerac (1950 and 1990)
The Three Musketeers (numerous versions)

The Restoration/Baroque Era

Barry Lyndon (1975)
The Libertine (2004)
The Man in the Iron Mask (1977 and 1998)
Restoration (1995)
Stage Beauty (2004)

The Georgian/Rococo Period

The Affair of the Necklace (2004)
Amadeus (1984)
Dangerous Liasons (1988)

The Duchess (2008)
The Madness of King George (1994)
Marie Antoinette (1938 and 2006)
The Patriot (2000)

The Regency/Empire Period

The Count of Monte Cristo (several versions)
Les Misérables (several versions)
Pride and Prejudice (numerous versions)
Vanity Fair (2004)

Wig Styling Resources

This is a listing of the suppliers I use most frequently in wig-making projects. I like the products they sell and have had good luck with their service.

1 **Hairess Corporation**
   880 Industrial Blvd
   Crown Point IN 46307
   (219)662-1060
   www.hairess.com

   Hairess is an excellent one-stop shopping place for wig-styling needs. It carries everything—wig steamers, canvas heads, wig clamps, Styrofoam heads, combs, brushes, scissors, pins, elastics, wig caps, wig-styling products—really, almost everything you could need. Be aware that there is a minimum order and that some items can only be purchased in bulk.

2 **Sally Beauty Supply**
   Stores nationwide
   www.sallybeauty.com

   Sally's carries a broad selection of combs, brushes, styling products, styling tools, hair nets, pins, colored hairsprays, and hair dyes.

3 **De Meo Brothers**
   2 Brighton Ave
   Passaic NJ 07055
   (973) 778-8100
   www.demeobrothers.com

   De Meo Brothers sells wig-making supplies primarily. This is where you can purchase wig laces, ventilating needles and holders, drawing cards, and human hair.

4 **Wilshire Wigs**
   5241 Craner Ave
   North Hollywood CA 91601
   1-800-927-0874
   www.wilshirewigs.com

   Wilshire Wigs is an excellent source for all manner of wigs. It carries a huge variety of brands, and many synthetic and human hair wigs. It also offers many hairpieces (good for taking apart and making into other things), and some extension hair/wefting. I buy the Giant, Wig America, and Look of Love brands most often. Specific wigs that I find most useful are:

   • the "Ashley" wig by Giant: this long, one length wig comes in a huge range of colors, including white, several different colors of gray, and bright party colors;

   • the "Angela" wig by Giant: a nice shoulder-length wig, again available in a ton of colors;

   • "Cassie" and "Christine" by Wig America: this is a reasonably priced long wig (Cassie is curly and Christine is straight) that comes in a nice range of colors (these come in white, but not gray);

   • "Dolly" by Wig America: a great base wig to create the Hedgehog style because it has lots of long, fluffy layers;

- "Lily" by Wig America: this wig is a good wig that is shoulder length, and is good for styles like 1940s women and Cavalier men that require a medium-length wig;

- the "Fingerwave Wig" in the 1920s, 30s and 40s costume category is a nice little classic wig that comes styled and works great in a pinch.

5   **International Wig**
    Hairs to Wigs
    848 N. Rainbow Blvd, Suite 4557
    Las Vegas NV 89107
    1-800-790-5013
    www.internationalwigs.com

International Wigs has a huge selection of wigs and hairpieces. I really like their selection of weaving and braiding hair and use it frequently to both add to existing wigs and to build wigs from scratch.

6   **Wow Wigs**
    P.O. Box 3054
    Cerritos CA 90703
    1-714-228-9627
    www.wowwigs.com

Wow Wigs is another company with a huge range of wigs, hairpieces, and weaving/braiding hair.

The wigs I order most often from the Sepia brand are:

- the "Ashley" wig, which is reasonably priced and comes in a nice range of colors;

- the "Nicole" wig, which is a bit longer than the Ashley wig, and also comes in a nice range of colors, especially blondes;

- the "LA4000," which is a good quality, waist-length wig. The color range is limited, but it does come in white.

- **His and Her Hair Goods Co.**
  5525 Wilshire Blvd
  Los Angeles CA 90036

1-800-421-4417
www.hisandher.com

This is another excellent source for weaving and braiding hair. It also carries a decent selection of wig laces and nets. Its textured hair for African-Americans is particularly good.

7   **M&J Trimming**
    1008 Sixth Avenue
    (Between 37th and 38th Str)
    New York NY 10018
    www.mjtrim.com

This trimming store is a good place to buy beads, ribbons, braids, and all sorts of other decorative objects that can be used to make hair decorations.

8   **Hats by Leko**
    P.O. Box 170
    Odell OR 97044
    www.hatsupply.com

This hat supply store is a good source for millinery wire (for making wig frames), horsehair, hat bases, tiaras, ribbons, veiling/netting, and flowers (really lovely ones for hair decoration purposes).

9   **I Kick Shins**
    www.ikickshins.net

This website is a great source for all manner of funky hair things. It carries artificial dreadlocks, tubular crin for making cyberlox, strips of foam, feather extensions, and everything else you might need to make a custom anime, cosplay, or cyber look.

10 **Hair Boutique**
    (866) 469-4247
    http://mp.hairboutique.com

This website carries an absurd variety of hair accessories.

11 **Japanese Style**
    1-877-226-4387
    www.japanesestyle.com

This website has a small but nice selection of kanzashi (Japanese hair ornaments).

<h1>{ Index }</h1>